dishy desserts

dishy desserts

KYLE BOOKS

This edition published in 2004 by Kyle Books,
an imprint of Kyle Cathie Limited.
general.enquiries@kyle-cathie.com
www.kylecathie.com

Distributed by National Book Network
4501 Forbes Blvd., Suite 200
Lanham, MD 20706
Phone: (301) 459 3366
Fax: (301) 429 5746

ISBN 1-904920-09-8

Text © see page 176
Photographs © see page 176

The Library of Congress Cataloguing-in-Publication
Data is available on file.

Printed and bound in China by C & C Offset
Printing Co., Ltd.

contents

introduction

For many people, desserts are the part of the meal we most look forward to. Even the simplest of fresh fruit salads rounds off a meal in a satisfying way, and a really special creation can be the crowning glory of a dinner party.

Desserts all too often fall by the wayside, condemned as being too time-consuming to prepare in our busy lives. And in these health- and weight-conscious days, many people allow themselves a dessert only on special occasions, as a particular treat. But desserts need not be complicated in order to taste good. This book shows that there are desserts for every occasion, from the simplest poached fruit that can be served any night of the week with no more than 10 minutes preparation, to more complex recipes that really push the boat out.

Sometimes it can be harder to choose what to cook than actually to cook it. Follow some simple principles and you can't go wrong. Try to choose seasonal produce - strawberries in summer are so much better than the pale imitations available in the shops in the depths of winter. (Although if you have a sudden urge for steamed pudding during a heatwave, don't deny yourself!) Think too about what has gone before in the meal. If you're serving a simple piece of broiled fish or meat for the main course, a luscious slice of tart or chocolate fondant might go down well. If you have served a heavy main course, it might be better to finish with a sorbet, or fresh fruit. Anything involving chocolate always seems to go down well - no matter what has gone before, everyone somehow manages to eat it!

If you are cooking for guests, take some time to plan your menu. If you know you won't have much time to spend in the kitchen on the night, choose a dessert that can be prepared in advance and left in the fridge or freezer until it's needed. If you're planning a casual supper where everyone chips in, you can plan a dessert that can be prepared at the last minute. If you are serving a cheese course, the jury's out as to whether you should serve cheese before dessert or the other way round. British tradition is to offer dessert before cheese but you might prefer to follow the continental example and finish on something sweet instead.

Presentation is important where desserts are concerned. Remember that we all 'eat with our eyes' before the food even gets to our plate and a beautifully presented pudding will be the crowning glory of any meal. Try adding a dusting of icing sugar over a simple fruit compote or placing a sprig of mint in a bowl of luscious red strawberries. A plain cake can be transformed into a magnificent gâteau with the addition of whipped cream and piled fruit. Chocolate curls add sophistication to ice creams and chocolate coffee beans make a statement on a mousse or fondant.

Always try to choose the best-quality produce for your desserts. Choosing the freshest fruit and using chocolate with a high cocoa content will make a real difference to the finished product. Most of the ingredients used in these recipes - even produce which would have been considered exotic a few years ago is on sale in the produce section of most supermarkets. Other ingredients might take a little more effort to track down but many can be found in Asian or Caribbean stores or markets.

tips & shortcuts

use your freezer

Many varieties of fruit are now available in frozen form nowadays, and make a good standby for quickly prepared desserts. Top frozen fruit with crumble mixture and bake for a quick family pudding, or make a fruit compote by warming the fruit with red wine, sugar and vanilla seeds. Serve with sour cream for a fresh and satisfying dessert.

convenience foods

Pastry is not difficult to make, but if you simply don't have the time, there are various products found in most supermarkets that will make your life easier. Phyllo, sweet and puff pastry are all available. For a quick pudding, simply roll out squares of puff pastry, top with fresh fruit and a dusting of sugar and bake for a few minutes. Phyllo pastry can be made into little purse shapes, or laid on top of fruit in a pie dish to add the satisfying crunch of pastry without the same calorific content.

healthy desserts

All of us should be aiming to eat at least 5 portions of fruit and vegetables per day. A portion counts as a slice of melon, an apple, or half a grapefruit, 3 tablespoons of cooked vegetables such as peas, sweetcorn, or carrots, or a cereal-bowl of salad. The health-giving benefits of increasing fruit and vegetables consumption are generally recognised. A fruit-based dessert can go to make up part of those five portions a day, so there's really no reason to deprive yourself!

how to use this book

Each recipe provides information about the number of servings it provides, and how long it takes to prepare and cook. As a general principle, the preparation time is the time it takes to wash, prepare, and chop the ingredients for the recipe, and the cooking time is the time you actually need to spend cooking, although for much of this time the dish may be able to be left to its own devices while you get on with something else.

In addition, each recipe provides nutritional information. As a rough guide, children, sedentary women, and older adults need approximately 1,600 calories per day. Teenage girls, active women, and sedentary men need 2,200 calories, and teenage boys, active men, and very active women need up to 2,800 per day.

There is information about the amount of fats per serving. Current advice is that no more than 10-30 per cent of our daily energy intake should come from fats. Most of us should be trying to cut down on total fats, particularly saturated fats. Carbohydrates are given next - they are an important part of everyone's diet. It is recommended that at least a third of our daily intake is made up of starchy foods such as potatoes, yams, bread, pasta, noodles, chapattis, rice, sweet potatoes, and so on.

It is recommended that our daily salt intake not exceed 6g. Most of us consume more like 9g (the equivalent of 2 teaspoonfuls). Much of the salt we consume comes from processed convenience foods, but approximately 10 per cent of it comes from salt we add to our food, either during cooking or at the table. High salt consumption is implicated in raised blood pressure, which is turn has been linked to a higher risk of heart disease and stroke.

fruit-based desserts

mango soufflé with lime sabayon

4-6 mangoes, peeled and diced

3 tablespoons water

juice and rind of 3 limes

5 egg whites

4 tablespoons superfine sugar, plus extra for
  dusting

butter for greasing

Lime sauce

3 limes

3 tablespoons light brown sugar

2 tablespoons unsalted butter

3/4 cup heavy cream

Place the mangoes in a pan with the water over gentle heat. Simmer for 5 minutes. Add the lime juice and rind. Purée in a food processor and set aside.

Preheat the oven to 350°F.

Beat the egg whites in a large bowl and gently add the superfine sugar. With a metal spoon fold the mango purée into the egg mixture. Butter 4 medium-sized soufflé dishes and dust with superfine sugar, making sure the dishes are completely coated. Gently pour in the mango mixture and lightly smooth the top. Cook the soufflés for 25 minutes, or until the top has browned and risen.

For the sauce, shred the rind of 2 limes. Mix the rind with the juice of all 3 limes and pour into a small saucepan. Add the brown sugar and cook over a low heat until the sugar has dissolved. Add the butter and allow to melt, then pour in the cream and stir thoroughly. Bring the sauce to a boil, and let it bubble for 2 minutes until the cream has thickened. Pour the sauce into a jug.

Serve the soufflés immediately they are ready, with the sauce.

Nutritional value per serving:

Calories: 408

Fats: 30g

Carbohydrates: 32g

Salt: 0.27g

nectarines with honey & sauternes

$^1/_2$ cup superfine sugar

1 tablespoon small mint leaves, stalks removed

4 large nectarines

2 tablespoons unsalted butter

5 tablespoons lavender honey

shredded rind of $^1/_4$ lemon

$^1/_2$ teaspoon lavender pollen (see TIP)

$^1/_3$ cup Sauternes or other sweet dessert wine

4 tablespoons slivered almonds, lightly toasted

Combine the sugar with 2 cups of water in a saucepan and bring slowly to a boil, stirring to dissolve the sugar. Add the stalks from the mint leaves, then the nectarines and simmer for 5 minutes, turning the nectarines occasionally if the liquid doesn't cover them completely. Remove from the heat and set aside. When the nectarines are cool enough to handle, peel them, cut in half and remove the pits. Return the nectarine halves to the cooked syrup (this may all be done well in advance).

To serve, melt the butter in a large skillet and stir in the honey, lemon rind, and lavender pollen. Drain the nectarines, toss them in the honey mixture, and then pour in the Sauternes. Turn the nectarines in the pan until glazed all over. Place the nectarines on serving plates, coat with the lavender honey sauce, scatter over the toasted almonds and mint leaves and serve.

TIP

Lavender pollen is the name given to ground lavender flowers. To make, simply dry the flowers, then place in a mortar or blender and blitz to a fine powder. Use to flavor all manner of dishes: for instance add to pasta with chopped parsley and walnuts, or to ricotta with lemon and lime rind and cream to make a wonderful mousse.

Nutritional value per serving:

Calories: 342

Fats: 11g

Carbohydrates: 56g

Salt: 0.03g

spicy papaya
& melon salad

juice of 1-2 limes
6 tablespoons sugar
1 hot red chile
1-2 papayas, peeled, pitted and diced
1 small ripe melon, pitted and diced

Put the lime juice and sugar in a small saucepan with its own volume of water. Bring gently to a boil, stirring to dissolve the sugar crystals. Add the chile, remove from the heat, and leave to infuse and cool. Combine the prepared fruits in a bowl and dress with the sugar syrup. Top with the infused chile as a warning to the unwary.

Nutritional value per serving:

Calories: 151

Fats: 0g

Carbohydrates: 37g

Salt: 0.04g

stuffed apples with **rhubarb crumble & lavender**

1$^{1}/_{4}$lb rhubarb, chopped

juice and shredded rind of 1 orange

$^{1}/_{2}$ cup demerara sugar

1 teaspoon ground cinnamon

4 Golden Delicious apples

1$^{1}/_{4}$ cups all-purpose flour

1 teaspoon baking powder

$^{1}/_{2}$ cup demerara sugar

1 teaspoon lavender pollen (see page 16)

$^{3}/_{4}$ cup blanched almonds, chopped (optional)

6 tablespoons unsalted butter, diced

1 teaspoon lavender flowers, to decorate

Put the rhubarb, orange juice and rind, sugar, and cinnamon in a saucepan and bring to a boil. Cover and simmer for 8-10 minutes, then cool slightly.

Cut the tops off the apples, about $^{3}/_{4}$in from the top, and with a small teaspoon carefully scoop out the core and pips. Fill the apples with the rhubarb mixture.

Preheat the oven to 350°F. For the topping, sift the flour and baking powder into a bowl and stir in the sugar, lavender pollen, and almonds, if using. Blend the butter into the flour mixture until it resembles breadcrumbs. Sprinkle the crumble mixture over the apples, pressing down lightly to form a crust.

Place the apples in a buttered ovenproof dish and bake for 35-40 minutes, until they are tender and the crumble is golden and crisp. Decorate with the lavender flowers and serve with lashings of cream or good old custard.

Nutritional value per serving:

Calories: 598

Fats: 27g

Carbohydrates: 85g

Salt: 0.42g

baked almond-stuffed **peaches**

4 peaches

3$\frac{1}{2}$oz amaretti biscuits, crumbled

1 egg

2 tablespoons roughly chopped blanched whole
   almonds

2 tablespoons light brown sugar

butter, for greasing

Preheat the oven to 350°F. Halve the peaches and remove the pits. Combine the amaretti, egg, almonds, and sugar. Stuff the peaches with this mixture.

Generously butter an ovenproof dish and arrange the peaches in it, cut-sides up. Pour in $\frac{2}{3}$ cup of water and bake, uncovered, in the preheated oven for 30 minutes, or until the peaches are tender but short of collapsing.

Nutritional value per serving:

Calories: 251

Fats: 10g

Carbohydrates: 38g

Salt: 0.36g

mango & passion fruit trifle

8 amaretti biscuits, roughly broken

4 slices panettone

8 tablespoons very sweet thick sherry

2 mangoes, peeled and roughly chopped

4 passion fruit

$2/3$ cup cream for whipping

3 tablespoons superfine sugar

Put half the crushed amaretti into the bottom of 4 glasses. Break the panettone up into bite-sized pieces and divide equally among the 4 glasses. Drizzle a tablespoon of sherry into each one.

Add the chopped mango to the glasses, together with the pulp scooped out of the passion fruit.

Whip the cream with the sugar until standing in soft peaks, fold in the remaining sherry and spoon over the top of the other ingredients.

Top with the remaining amaretti biscuits and serve.

Nutritional value per serving:

Calories: 565

Fats: 24g

Carbohydrates: 77g

Salt: 0.46g

poached plums

3/4 cup sugar

1 cup cold water

12 large fresh plums, pitted

Put the sugar and water into a saucepan and bring slowly to a boil. Add the plums; cover and simmer until the plums are soft and bursting. Turn into a bowl and serve chilled with pouring cream.

TIP

Try substituting apricots for the plums.

Nutritional value per serving:

Calories: 235

Fats: 0g

Carbohydrates: 62g

Salt: 0.02g

pears in honey & saffron

4 firm pears

2 heaped tablespoons honey

juice of 1 lemon

1 cup water

1 stick cinnamon

2 cloves

1 teaspoon saffron strands

Peel the pears, leaving the stalks intact. Put the honey and lemon juice in a heavy saucepan into which the pears will fit snugly and place over a moderate heat. Stir until the honey has melted then add the water and spices. Keep stirring until the liquid comes to a boil then turn down the heat and leave to simmer for 5 minutes. Now add the pears to the liquid and simmer for 20 minutes, turning carefully halfway through and basting the pears regularly with the sauce. Leave the pears to cool in the syrup before serving.

Nutritional value per serving:

Calories: 108

Fats: 0g

Carbohydrates: 27g

Salt: 0.03g

SERVES 4

PREPARATION TIME: 20 MINUTES

COOKING TIME: 2 MINUTES

FREEZING TIME: 1 HOUR

pavlova with frozen raspberry yogurt

whites of 6 eggs
1²/₃ cups caster sugar
vegetable oil, for brushing

Frozen raspberry yogurt
2 boxes of raspberries
4 tablespoons sugar
2 drops of vanilla essence
1 teaspoon lemon juice
2 egg yolks
2 cups plain runny yogurt

First make the frozen raspberry yogurt: put the raspberries in a large saucepan with the sugar and vanilla essence, 2 tablespoons of water and the lemon juice. Bring to a boil, purée, and allow to cool. Fill another saucepan one-third full of water and bring to a boil, then reduce to simmer. Put the egg yolks and a teaspoon of water in a heatproof bowl and place over the pan. Whisk the egg yolks until pale and fluffy, remove from the heat, and continue to whisk for another 30 seconds. Fold two-thirds of the cooled raspberry purée into the egg yolk mix and add the yogurt. Fold together and place in an ice-cream machine for 40–60 minutes.

Make the pavlova: turn your oven on at the lowest possible setting. Bring another saucepan half-filled with water to a boil and again place a clean bowl over it. After 2 minutes, remove the warmed bowl and pour the egg whites into it. Whisk vigorously, adding the sugar slowly, a tablespoon at a time, into the egg whites. Continue whisking until the egg whites are firm and peaking with a glossy sheen. Place waxed paper on 2 oven sheets and brush with oil. Put 6 dollops of the meringue mixture on to each sheet, leaving at least 3in between each. Place in the oven for 1³/₄–2 hours.

Once the meringues are cooked (when tapped gently they sound hollow), remove from the oven and allow to cool. When they are cool, use a bread knife to cut each meringue in half like a roll. Take curled scoops of your iced yogurt by dragging a dessertspoon over the yogurt's surface, place one in the middle of each meringue base, pop the top back on and press down gently. Once all of the meringues are stuffed, pour the remaining raspberry purée over their tops and serve on a large dish.

Nutritional value per serving:
Calories: 538
Fats: 5g
Carbohydrates: 119g
Salt: 0.5g

strawberry tiramisu

1$^{1}/_{2}$ cups mascarpone cheese

18 (about 6oz) boudoir sponge fingers

1 cup sweet dessert wine (Sauternes or similar)

1 cup strawberries, hulled

1 cup heavy cream

Spoon half of the mascarpone on to the bottom of a serving bowl. Pour the wine into a shallow dish and dip in the sponge fingers before arranging them over the mascarpone, breaking them up as necessary.

Cover with half the strawberries and then spread the rest of the mascarpone on the top, smoothing down the top with a palette knife that has been briefly dipped in boiling water. Chill for at least two hours or overnight.

To serve, scatter over the remaining strawberries and bring to the table for maximum effect. Spoon into glass dishes to serve.

Nutritional value per serving:

Calories: 579

Fats: 45g

Carbohydrates: 33g

Salt: 0.27g

SERVES 8

PREPARATION TIME: 20 MINUTES

COOKING TIME: 1 HOUR

FREEZING TIME: 1 HOUR

strawberry sundae

2 egg whites

pinch of salt

$2/3$ cup superfine sugar

2 cups strawberries, cleaned, hulled,
    and halved

juice of half a lemon

confectioners' sugar to taste

1 cup cream for whipping

To assemble

$2/3$ cup cream for whipping

8 large strawberries

8 sprigs of mint

Preheat the oven to 250°F. Line two baking sheets with baking parchment.

Place the egg whites in a large bowl along with the salt. Using an electric beater, whisk into stiff peaks. Add half the superfine sugar and continue whisking until thick and glossy, 2-3 minutes. Add the remaining sugar in a steady stream whilst continually beating. Fill the meringue into a piping bag fitted with a medium-sized nozzle. Pipe 2in meringues evenly spaced onto the baking parchment. You will have approximately 24 meringues. Bake in the preheated oven for 45 minutes. Turn off the oven and allow the meringues to cool inside. Store in an airtight container until required.

Place the strawberries in a blender or food processor along with the lemon juice. Process until roughly chopped then add the confectioners' sugar. Process for a few seconds more. You will have about $3^{1}/2$ cups of purée.

Reserve $1^{1}/4$ cups of the purée and refrigerate until required. Place the remainder in the bowl of an ice-cream maker with the cream. Churn until frozen. Transfer to a freezeproof container and freeze until required.

Chill eight tall glasses on a tray in the fridge for 15 minutes. Lightly whip the remaining cream to soft peaks. Place a small scoop of ice cream in the base of each glass, add a crushed meringue, top with a spoonful of cream and a drizzle of the reserved strawberry purée. Repeat with two more layers of each. Place a strawberry and a sprig of mint or borage on top of each sundae and serve immediately with long spoons.

Nutritional value per serving:

Calories: 278

Fats: 20g

Carbohydrates: 24g

Salt: 0.23g

two-pepper red wine strawberries

$^2/_3$ cup good-quality red wine, preferably
   Cabernet Sauvignon

4 tablespoons superfine sugar

$^1/_2$ teaspoon black peppercorns,
   coarsely cracked

2in piece of vanilla pod

1 teaspoon cornstarch

2 tablespoons unsalted butter

1$^1/_4$ cups strawberries

$^1/_2$ teaspoon green peppercorns, drained

vanilla ice cream, to serve

mint leaves, to decorate

Put the wine in a saucepan, holding back 2 tablespoons of it, and add the sugar and half the black pepper. Add the vanilla seeds, and the pod, and stir over a moderate heat to dissolve the sugar. Bring to a boil. Mix the 2 tablespoons of wine with the cornstarch and add to the pan. Cook gently for 1-2 minutes, until the mixture has thickened slightly. Remove the sauce from the heat and take out the vanilla pod.

Melt the butter in a skillet over a high heat, add the strawberries and the remaining black pepper and cook for 1 minute. Pour over the wine sauce and return to a boil. Add the green peppercorns, then pour into a bowl and leave to cool. Refrigerate overnight to allow the flavors to develop. To serve, put the strawberry mixture in cocktail glasses, top with vanilla ice cream and decorate with mint leaves.

How to remove vanilla seeds

To remove the seeds from a vanilla pod, make a slit along the length of the pod with a sharp knife then carefully run the tip of the knife from one end of the slit to the other.

Nutritional value per serving:

Calories: 168

Fats: 5g

Carbohydrates: 24g

Salt: 0.03g

mixed berries with
champagne sabayon

1¹/₄ cups Champagne

4 tablespoons superfine sugar

4 egg yolks

3¹/₂oz blackberries

3¹/₂oz raspberries

3¹/₂oz redcurrants, stalks removed

Place the Champagne in a saucepan with the sugar and simmer for a few minutes until the sugar dissolves, stirring occasionally. Remove from the heat and allow to cool a little.Place the egg yolks in a large heatproof bowl set over a saucepan of simmering water and whisk until well combined and just heated through. Gradually pour in the Champagne mixture, a little at a time until completely combined, whisking continuously.

Continue to whisk the sabayon until the mixture has doubled in size, being careful not to allow the mixture to become too hot or the sabayon may split – this should take no more than 6-8 minutes. Remove the bowl from the heat and allow to cool.

To serve, preheat the broiler until it is very hot. Arrange the berries in a wide-rimmed dish and spoon over enough of the sabayon to just cover. Place under the grill for a few minutes until golden. Serve immediately.

TIP

Sabayon is a classic French sauce and once you get the hang of it, it's a doddle to make. It will keep happily for a couple of hours, covered with plastic wrap in the fridge, but after that it starts to lose some of its volume.

Nutritional value per serving:

Calories: 184

Fats: 6g

Carbohydrates: 20g

Salt: 0.04g

warm **berries** on toasted panettone with heavy cream

6 tablespoons redcurrant jelly

juice of 1 lemon

1-2 tablespoons brandy

4 slices of panettone

$1/4$ cup strawberries

$1/3$ cup blueberries

$1/3$ cup blackberries

$1/3$ cup raspberries

confectioners' sugar for dusting

heavy cream, to serve

Gently melt the redcurrant jelly with the lemon juice and brandy in a skillet. Meanwhile, toast the panettone slices on both sides and keep warm.

When the jelly has melted and is well blended with the other ingredients, add all the berries and toss gently, coating the fruit.

Place the toasted panettone on serving plates, spoon on the hot fruit and dust with confectioners' sugar. Serve with a dollop of heavy cream.

Nutritional value per serving:

Calories: 391

Fats: 13g

Carbohydrates: 64g

Salt: 0.42g

champagne **berry** jello

unscented vegetable oil, for greasing

1 cup very small strawberries

1 cup redcurrants

1 cup whitecurrants

1 cup golden raspberries

1 cup blueberries

1 cup loganberies

10 leaves of gelatine

$^2/_3$ cup superfine sugar

$^2/_3$ cup water

1 bottle pink Champagne

Brush 10 tall jello molds (holding about $^2/_3$ cup) with a little unscented vegetable oil. Pick over the fruit, wash, and dry well. Soak gelatine as shown below. In a saucepan, bring the sugar and water to a boil. Reduce the heat and simmer for about 5 minutes to form a clear syrup. Remove from the heat. Squeeze out excess water from the gelatine then dissolve it in the syrup. Add the Champagne, stir and strain through a fine strainer into a large jug. Place the jello molds onto a tray that will fit inside your fridge. Pour in enough jello to coat the base of the molds – about $^1/_4$in. Leave to set in the fridge. When set, remove from the fridge and half-fill the molds with fruit. Pour in enough jello to cover three quarters of the fruit (any more and the fruit will float). Leave to set in the refrigerator, then fill to the top with the remaining jello to encase the fruit entirely. Leave to set in the fridge. Serve with pistachio ice-cream or biscuits.

How to soak gelatine leaves

Gelatine can come in small stiff transparent sheets - soak them in cold water until they become soft, then squeeze out the excess water and continue with recipe.

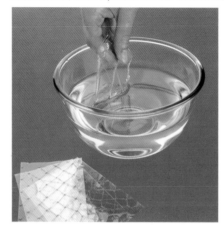

Nutritional value per serving:

Calories: 185

Fats: 2g

Carbohydrates: 27g

Salt: 0.08g

blackcurrant leaf sorbet

1$^{1}/_{3}$ cups superfine sugar

2$^{1}/_{2}$ cups water

rind and juice of 1 lemon

3 handfuls of blackcurrant leaves

Combine the sugar and water in a large saucepan. Add the lemon rind and stir over a gentle heat until the sugar has dissolved. Turn up the heat and allow the syrup to boil for 5 minutes. Remove from the heat and add the blackcurrant leaves and lemon juice. Cover with a lid and leave to infuse for 30 minutes. Strain through a strainer lined with a square of damp cheesecloth. Pour into the bowl of an ice-cream machine and churn until frozen. Transfer to a freezerproof container and freeze until required.

Serve in small scoops in well-chilled glasses.

TIP

Select young blackcurrant leaves as these give a fresh taste, and do not allow them to infuse for longer than half an hour as the resulting syrup may be sour and inedible.

Nutritional value per serving:

Calories: 273

Fats: 0g

Carbohydrates: 73g

Salt: 0.01g

SERVES 6-8

PREPARATION TIME: 10 MINUTES

COOKING TIME: 40 MINUTES

CHILLING TIME: 6-12 HOURS

gooseberry & elderflower charlotte

1 sachet gelatine ($^1/_2$oz)

2 tablespoons water

2 cups gooseberries, topped and tailed

$^1/_3$ cup superfine sugar

2 tablespoons elderflower cordial/syrup

2 tablespoons water

1 strip lemon rind

18 sponge fingers

1 dessertspoon elderflower cordial/syrup
   diluted with 2 tablespoons water

1$^1/_4$ cups heavy cream

1$^1/_4$ cups cream cheese

$^1/_2$ cup superfine sugar

2 tablespoons water

2 egg whites

$^2/_3$ cup whipped cream

elderflower heads, to decorate

Nutritional value per serving:

Calories: 588

Fats: 36g

Carbohydrates: 60g

Salt: 0.23g

Sprinkle the gelatine over the water in a small ramekin. Place the gooseberries in a large saucepan with the sugar, elderflower cordial/syrup, water, and lemon rind. Cover and cook very gently for 5-6 minutes until soft. Don't worry if the fruits break up slightly. Add the soaked gelatine and stir to dissolve. Cool slightly, then press through a nylon strainer. Set aside and do not allow to set.

Brush the unsugared side of the sponge fingers with a little of the diluted elderflower cordial and use to line the sides of a 2 pint charlotte tin. Whip the cream to soft peaks and fold in the cream cheese. Fold into the cooled gooseberry purée.

Place the sugar and water in a heavy saucepan. Cook over a low heat until the sugar dissolves. Wash down the sides of the pan with a clean brush dipped in cold water. Bring to a boil and insert a sugar thermometer. After 1 minute place the egg whites in a large bowl and whisk to stiff peaks. When the syrup reaches the soft ball stage on the sugar thermometer 240°F, remove from the heat and pour in a thin, steady stream on to the egg whites while continually whisking. Continue whisking until the meringue is cold, thick, and glossy.

Stir a couple of spoonfuls of the meringue into the gooseberry mixture to loosen it. Then fold in the remainder. Carefully spoon the mousse into the prepared charlotte tin. Refrigerate for several hours or overnight. To turn out, turn the point of a knife round the top edge of the charlotte. Dip the mold briefly into a basin of hot water, invert onto a serving plate and the dessert will slide out. Decorate with whipped cream and elderflower heads.

berry trifle

3 large macaroons

4 tablespoons sherry or brandy

4 tablespoons blueberry or blackberry jelly

1½ cups fruits such as blueberries, blackberries, or wild raspberries, washed and dried

1¼ cups marscapone

4 tablespoons sugar

1-2 tablespoons milk

1¾ cups milk

1 vanilla pod, split

1 whole egg

3 egg yolks

3 tablespoons superfine sugar

⅓ cup all-purpose flour

⅓ cup cream for whipping

a few extra berries, to decorate

Cut each macaroon into six pieces and lay in a large glass serving bowl, or divide between 4 small glass dishes. Spoon over the sherry or brandy. Warm the jelly and spread over the macaroons. Pile the washed and dried fruits on top.

Combine the marscapone with the sugar and enough milk to give a soft consistency. Spread evenly over the fruits. Chill in the refrigerator.

Combine the milk and split vanilla pod in a saucepan and bring to a boil. Whisk the whole egg, egg yolks, and sugar until thick and pale. Stir in the flour. Pour a little of the boiling milk onto the eggs, stir to blend, then return to the pan with the remainder of the milk. Cook, stirring, until the custard thickens and boiling point is reached. The flour will prevent the custard from curdling. Cook for 2 more minutes. Transfer to a clean bowl, dab the top with a little extra milk to prevent a skin forming, then set aside to cool. Whisk the custard to ensure it is smooth before spooning over the trifle.

Decorate with whipped cream and a few extra berries.

Nutritional value per serving:

Calories: 527

Fats: 34g

Carbohydrates: 47g

Salt: 0.3g

cherry clafoutis

Cherry compote
4 tablespoons superfine sugar
2lb fresh cherries, pitted
3 tablespoons kirsch

Clafoutis batter
$1/2$ stick butter, melted
4 tablespoons superfine sugar to coat molds
6 large eggs
$1^1/_3$ cups superfine sugar
$1^1/_2$ cups all-purpose flour, sifted
$1^1/_4$ cups heavy cream
$1^1/_4$ cups full-fat milk
2 tablespoons kirsch
confectioners' sugar, to dust

In a saucepan gently heat the sugar in 1 tablespoon of water until dissolved. Add the cherries and kirsch, and cook on a low heat for 15 minutes, or until the cherries are soft but still whole. Remove from the heat. Drain half the cherries, leaving the rest in the liquid.

Preheat the oven to 350°F. Oil the inside of a large baking dish with melted butter and superfine sugar, then put aside. In a mixer, whisk the eggs until frothy, add sugar; then whisk for a further 2 minutes. Add the flour, cream, milk, and kirsch, then whisk until well blended. Place the drained, cooked cherries in the baking dish, pour over the batter and place on a baking sheet. Bake for 15 minutes then remove the clafoutis from the oven and top up with any remaining batter. Return to the oven for 15 minutes until the clafoutis is golden in color and firm to touch.

Remove, dust with confectioners' sugar, and place on plates with a spoonful of compote. Serve.

TIP
A sweet white dessert wine such as Muscat Beaume de Venise goes perfectly with this traditional French baked pudding.

Nutritional value per serving:
Calories: 489
Fats: 20g
Carbohydrates: 70g
Salt: 0.37g

apple pecorino strudel

3/4 cup fresh white breadcrumbs

1/2 cup ground almonds

1 stick unsalted butter

7-8 medium cooking apples, peeled, cored and
thinly sliced

4 tablespoons superfine sugar

1 teaspoon ground cinnamon

1/2 teaspoon ground mixed spice

1/3 cup raisins, soaked in water until plump

1/4 cup walnuts or almonds, chopped

rind of half a lemon

5oz Pecorino Romano, thinly sliced

4 large sheets of phyllo pastry, about 18 x 12in

confectioners' sugar, for dusting

Preheat the oven to 400°F. Fry the breadcrumbs and ground almonds in half of the butter until lightly golden, then set aside.

Mix together the apples, sugar, cinnamon, mixed spice, raisins, nuts, and lemon rind. Carefully fold in the Pecorino cheese.

Melt the remaining butter. Lay out 1 sheet of phyllo dough on a work surface and brush with some of the butter, then top with the remaining sheets of phyllo, brushing with butter between the layers. Brush the final sheet of pastry with more butter and sprinkle the fried breadcrumb mixture over the top. Spread the apple mixture over the surface and roll up the pastry to form a compact roll. Transfer to a greased baking sheet, curving the strudel to fit if necessary, and brush with the remaining melted butter. Bake for 20-25 minutes, until crisp and golden.

Remove from the oven, dust generously with confectioners' sugar and serve hot.

TIP

Ricotta makes a tasty alternative to the Pecorino.

Nutritional value per serving:

Calories: 533

Fats: 31g

Carbohydrates: 51g

Salt: 1.34g

passion fruit pyramid

Meringue

12 egg whites

2¹/₂ cups superfine sugar

Passion fruit cream

30 whole passion fruit, halved, juices and pips
    scooped out, sifted to yield ³/₄ cup purée

1 cup water

3¹/₄ cups heavy cream

1¹/₄ cups sugar

¹/₃ cup cornstarch

10 egg yolks

1¹/₂ sticks unsalted butter, cut into cubes

3 passion fruit

8 mangos, peeled and sliced

Garnish

confectioners' sugar

6 passion fruit

edible flowers, such as violets, fresh or
    crystallized

Nutritional value per serving:

Calories: 515

Fats: 29g

Carbohydrates: 62g

Salt: 0.17g

Preheat the oven to 225°F. Taking four sheets of silicone paper, draw a 12in circle on the first, on the second a 10in circle, on the third a 8in circle and on the fourth a 6in circle. Place these papers on baking sheets. Whisk the egg whites with ¹/₂ cup of the sugar until it forms stiff peaks. Continue to whisk, adding the sugar gradually. Once all the sugar is added, the egg whites should be stiff and glossy. Fill a piping bag with this mixture and pipe to fill each of the paper circles. Bake for 8-10 hours until the meringue is dry and hard to the touch, allow to cool, then layer with non-stick paper and store in airtight containers.

In a heavy saucepan, bring the passion fruit purée, the water, 4 tablespoons cream and the sugar to a boil, stirring continuously. Mix the cornstarch with a little cold water then add to the boiling mixture, stirring. Reduce the heat and cook for 5 minutes, stirring to prevent it from burning. Remove from heat and allow to cool for about 2 minutes. Beat in the egg yolks then the butter. Cover with non-stick paper and allow to cool. Cut the 3 passion fruit in half, squeeze out the juice and pips, and add these to the mixture. Whisk the remaining cream until it holds its shape and fold into the passion fruit.

Pipe a blob of cream in the center of a glass cake stand to prevent the meringue from sliding around. Place the largest disc of meringue on the stand and spread with cream, leaving a 1in rim of meringue. Top with a layer of mango, then the next meringue disc. Repeat the process twice to finish with the smallest disc of meringue. Dust with confectioners' sugar and arrange remaining slices of fresh or oven-dried mango on the top, squeezing over the juice of the 6 passion fruits. Decorate the sides with fresh or crystallized flowers.

lemon meringue pie

1/2 stick butter, plus more for oiling
1 pack of sweet shortcrust pastry
juice of 6 lemons and shredded rind of 4
1 tablespoon apricot jelly
9 egg yolks
1 cup superfine sugar
3/4 cup heavy cream
3 cups confectioners' sugar

Meringue
350g (12oz) caster sugar
whites of 6 eggs

TIP

If you like, you can make a lemon sauce for the
pie by straining 3-4 tablespoons of lemon
marmalade into a small saucepan, adding an
equal amount of water, and heating gently,
stirring, until syrupy.

Nutritional value per serving:
Calories: 698
Fats: 32g
Carbohydrates: 124g
Salt: 0.74g

Preheat the oven to 350°F and butter a 10in tart pan. Roll out the pastry to fit the pan, sprinkling with the rind of 1 lemon as you roll. Line the tart pan with the pastry and cover with a piece of waxed paper. Cover that with baking beans or dry rice and bake blind for 15-20 minutes until lightly colored. Remove from the oven and allow to cool, turning the oven setting down to 300°F.

While the tart shell is cooling, in a small saucepan mix the apricot jelly with 1 tablespoon of water and heat gently until you have a syrup (take care not to let it burn). Remove the beans or rice and paper from the tart shell and brush the pastry with the apricot syrup. Leave this to set while you make the filling.

Mix the egg yolks and superfine sugar together in a saucepan and bring to a gentle heat, then add the cream, lemon juice, and remaining rind, together with butter, stirring continuously so the mixture does not curdle. Pour the lemon mix into the cooled tart shell and place in the oven for 10 minutes. Once the tart is cooked, remove it from the oven and allow to cool.

While it cools, make the meringue: using a spotlessly clean bowl and whisk, put 1 tablespoon of the sugar in the bottom of the bowl, add the egg whites and beat vigorously until they are standing in soft peaks. Slowly add the remaining sugar, beating constantly, until the egg whites are standing in firm peaks.

Dust the cooled tart with confectioners' sugar, spoon over meringue mixture and place under the broiler for about 1 or 2 minutes, until the meringue browns slightly.

blueberry pancakes with sour cream

1 cup all-purpose flour

1 tablespoon superfine sugar

2 tablespoons heavy cream

2 eggs, separated

shredded rind of 1 lemon

1 cup milk

unsalted butter

$1/2$ cup blueberries

4-6 tablespoons maple syrup

4 tablespoons sour cream

Sift the flour into a bowl, mix in the sugar and make a well in the center. In a separate bowl mix the cream, egg yolks, lemon rind and milk. Pour into the well in the flour and mix thoroughly, using a small whisk or wooden spoon to make a smooth batter.

Whisk the egg whites until stiff. Gently spoon a third into the batter to loosen the texture, then fold in the rest.

Melt a small knob of butter in a 6in skillet. Pour in a quarter of the batter; the pancakes should not be more than $1/2$in thick. Sprinkle some blueberries on the surface. When small bubbles begin to break on the surface, flip the pancake over and and cook for another minute or two. Slide onto a warm plate, drizzle with maple syrup and keep warm.

Make 3 more pancakes. Serve each helping with a dollop of sour cream.

TIP

The secret of light pancakes is to leave the batter in the fridge for 30 minutes to rest before cooking.

Nutritional value per serving:

Calories: 330

Fats: 16g

Carbohydrates: 39g

Salt: 0.23g

banana fritters

1 cup all-purpose flour

1 cup coconut milk

$^1/_2$ teaspoon salt

$^1/_4$ cup granulated sugar

1 tablespoon white sesame seeds

6 small or 3 large unripe bananas (the skins just
   turning yellow)

vegetable oil for deep-frying

Combine the flour, coconut milk, salt, sugar and sesame seeds in a bowl and mix to form a smooth batter. Set aside.

If using small bananas, cut in half; if using large bananas, cut into 3 pieces. (You should end up with pieces about 3in long.) Cut each piece in half lengthways to give strips about $^1/_2$in thick.

Heat the oil in a deep-fryer to 400°F. Dip the banana strips in the batter, shake off any excess and lower into the hot oil. Fry until golden brown, then remove, drain on kitchen paper towels, and serve immediately.

Nutritional value per serving:

Calories: 568

Fats: 31g

Carbohydrates: 71g

Salt: 0.79g

SERVES 6-8

PREPARATION TIME: 30 MINUTES

COOKING TIME: 45 MINUTES

swiss chard & pear tart

3/4 cup raisins or golden raisins

2 tablespoons dark rum

2lb Swiss chard, stalks removed, leaves cooked,
   and finely chopped

1/2 cup pinenuts

3/4 cup confectioners' sugar, plus extra
   for dusting

3 pears, peeled, cored and diced

3 tablespoons cream cheese

shredded rind of 1 lemon

2 fresh eggs, beaten

Pastry

3 cups all-purpose flour

2 sticks unsalted butter, diced
   (at room temperature)

pinch of salt

1 cup confectioners' sugar, sifted

finely shredded rind of 1/2 lemon

1 fresh egg, beaten

For the pastry, sift the flour on to a work surface and make a well in the center. Put the butter, salt, sugar, and lemon rind in the well and then add the egg. With your fingertips, gradually bring the flour into the center, blending in the butter, until all the ingredients come together into a soft dough. Knead very lightly for 1 minute, until completely smooth, then form the dough into a ball. Wrap in plastic wrap and leave to rest in the refrigerator for 30 minutes.

Preheat the oven to 400°F. Roll out the pastry and use to line a 9in flan pan, reserving excess pastry for the top. Prick the base with a fork and chill while you prepare the filling.

Soak the raisins or golden raisins in the rum for 15 minutes, then place in a saucepan and heat gently until all the liquid has been absorbed. Place the Swiss chard leaves in a bowl with the raisins and all the remaining ingredients. Mix well, then spread the filling in the pastry case and cover the top with the remaining pastry. Seal the edges and make a few vents in the top.

Bake for 45 minutes, until golden brown, then allow to cool. Turn out of the pan, dust with confectioners' sugar and serve.

TIP

If you do not have time to make pastry, you can now buy some good-quality pre-baked pastry cases. Or use the same filling but top with buttered phyllo pastry.

Nutritional value per serving:

Calories: 829

Fats: 44g

Carbohydrates: 100g

Salt:0.76 g

fennel & caramelized banana stacks

½ stick unsalted butter, melted

8 sheets of phyllo pastry

4 tablespoons confectioners' sugar, plus extra
   for dusting

Fennel mousse

1 large fennel bulb, chopped

⅓ cup superfine sugar

4 fresh egg yolks

2 tablespoons custard powder

¼ vanilla pod

4 tablespoons Marie Brizard (or other anise
   liquor such as Pernod)

2 tablespoons heavy cream, semi-whipped

Caramelized bananas

⅔ cup superfine sugar

3 large bananas, peeled and cut into slices
   ¾in thick

⅓ cup Marie Brizard (or other anise
   liqueur such as Pernod)

Nutritional value per serving:

Calories: 879

Fats: 22g

Carbohydrates: 149g

Salt: 1.13g

First prepare the phyllo stacks. Preheat the oven to 350°F. Brush a baking sheet with melted butter. Place a sheet of phyllo on a work surface, brush with melted butter, then place another sheet on top. Brush with butter and sprinkle with a tablespoon of confectioners' sugar. Top with another sheet of phyllo and brush with butter. Add the fourth sheet, brush with butter and sprinkle with more confectioners' sugar. Repeat with remaining four sheets so you have two separate piles. Cut out six 3in circles from each stack, place on the baking sheet, and bake for 5-7 minutes until golden brown. Remove from oven and cool.

For the fennel mousse, put the fennel in a pan, add 3 tablespoons of the sugar and enough water to cover. Bring to a boil, reduce the heat and simmer for 20-25 minutes until tender. Blitz in a blender to make ½ cup purée. Put the egg yolks, the remaining sugar and the custard powder in a bowl and whisk until smooth. Scrape out the vanilla seeds. Heat the fennel purée, Marie Brizard, and vanilla seeds in a saucepan and then carefully pour on to the egg mixture, whisking as you do so. Return to the pan and cook for 3-4 minutes, stirring constantly, until thickened. Transfer to a large bowl and allow to cool, then whisk until smooth. Fold in the whipped cream.

For the caramelized bananas, heat the sugar in a heavy skillet over a high heat until it dissolves and forms a caramel. Add the bananas and cook for 1 minute. Pour in the Marie Brizard to form a light anise caramel. Allow to cool. To assemble, place a phyllo circle in the center of each serving plate, place a heaped spoonful of fennel mousse in the center and top with some caramelized banana. Put another phyllo circle on top and repeat the layers of fennel mousse and banana. Top with a third phyllo circle. Dust with a little confectioners' sugar, pour around some of the caramel and serve immediately.

exotic
delights

prickly pear with mango

4 prickly pears with their spikes rubbed off

1 orange, juice and rind

3 tablespoons fresh lime juice

1 tablespoon tequila (optional)

3 tablespoons runny honey

1 large mango or 2 smaller ones, diced

Place the orange juice and rind, lime juice, tequila, and honey in a small saucepan, bring to a boil and simmer for 10 minutes. Carefully remove the skin of the prickly pears – avoiding any little bumps which might conceal left-behind spines – and mash the flesh together with the juice mixture. Serve spooned over the diced mango.

Nutritional value per serving:

Calories: 118

Fats: 0g

Carbohydrates: 29g

Salt: 0.02g

SERVES 4

PREPARATION TIME: 10 MINUTES

COOKING TIME: 1½ HOURS

CHILLING TIME: 2-12 HOURS

pumpkin & pecan crème

1lb fresh pumpkin, seeds removed, sliced, skin
   left on
½ stick unsalted butter
¾ cup pecan nuts, plus extra for decoration
6 egg yolks
½ cup superfine sugar
2 cups heavy cream

Preheat the oven to 375°F. Smear half of the butter over the pumpkin flesh and roast for about 1 hour or until tender. Leave to cool, then scoop out the flesh and pass it through a fine strainer or vegetable mouli to give 5oz. Reduce the oven to 300°F. Toast the pecans in the oven for about 5 minutes, then remove and allow to cool. Place the egg yolks and sugar in a large bowl and whisk until light and fluffy. Place the cream in a saucepan and bring to a boil, then slowly whisk into the egg mixture. Finally fold in the pumpkin purée. Oil four 7fl oz ramekins with the remaining butter, then pour in the pumpkin mixture and top with the pecan halves. Place in a bain-marie and cover with aluminum foil. Bake for 40-45 minutes until each ramekin is slightly raised around the edges and just set. Remove the bain-marie from the oven and allow to cool completely, then cover each ramekin with plastic wrap and chill for at least 2 hours or overnight. Decorate with leftover nuts and serve.

How to purée vegetables

A vegetable mouli is a useful piece of kitchen equipment, allowing cooked vegetables, such as pumpkin or potatoes, to be puréed without turning them into a gluey mass.

Nutritional value per serving:

Calories: 1091

Fats: 105g

Carbohydrates: 27g

Salt: 0.16g

gold threads

10 jasmine flowers

1³/₄ cups water

10 eggs

1 tablespoon vegetable oil

4 cups granulated sugar

Sprinkle the jasmine flowers over the water and leave to infuse for 1 hour. Separate the egg yolks and reserve the whites. Whisk the yolks in a large bowl until thick and creamy, add the egg whites and oil and whisk to combine. Remove the jasmine flowers from the perfumed water and discard. Pour the water into a large saucepan and add the sugar. Heat gently, stirring to dissolve the sugar, then boil rapidly to form a thin syrup. To make the threads, fill your home-made strainer (see TIP, below) with the egg mixture and drizzle it in thin streams into the simmering sugar syrup, moving it in a circular motion to form nests of threads. Cook for 1 minute or until golden brown, then remove with a skewer and place on a metal tray to cool.

TIP

This Thai dish is often served at birthday parties or prepared as an offering to the monks on special anniversary days.

How to make a home-made strainer

To make a home-made strainer, clean an empty tin can thoroughly. Pierce six holes in the bottom with a hammer and nail and then fill with batter to make the threads.

Nutritional value per serving:

Calories: 1096

Fats: 16g

Carbohydrates: 236g

Salt: 0.47g

pomegranates served with cream

2 large pomegranates, prepared as below

2 cups sour cream or Greek yogurt, well chilled

$^1/_4$ cup granulated sugar

1 tablespoon orange blossom water or a few
   drops of vanilla extract

shredded rind of $^1/_2$ lemon

2 tablespoons slivered almonds

4 sprigs mint

Peel the pomegranates as shown below.

Combine the sour cream or yogurt with the sugar, orange blossom water, and the lemon rind, and mix well.

In each of 4 tall glasses arrange the pomegranate seed and cream mixture in alternate layers, finishing with cream. Sprinkle with almonds, decorate with a sprig of mint, and serve.

How to peel a pomegranate

Remove the top and base. Then, with a sharp knife, score through the outer peel so dividing the fruit into segments. With your hands prise the peel from the delicate seeds, being careful to remove all traces of the thin yellow skin, which is very bitter.

Nutritional value per serving:

Calories: 514

Fats: 42g

Carbohydrates: 28g

Salt: 0.33g

lemongrass, coconut, & vanilla pannacotta

1 vanilla pod

2 lemongrass stalks, outer layers removed

$1^1/_2$ cups heavy cream

$^2/_3$ cup unsweetened coconut milk

3 tablespoons superfine sugar

$1^1/_2$ gelatine leaves

assortment of exotic fruits (such as mango, papaya, lychee, and dragonfruit), peeled and diced, to serve

Passionfruit-chile syrup

2 passionfruit, halved

$^1/_2$ cup stock syrup (see TIP)

juice and shredded rind of $^1/_2$ a lime

$^1/_8$ teaspoon pitted and finely diced red chile

Cut the vanilla pod in half lengthways and scrape out the seeds with the tip of a sharp knife. Bruise the lemongrass and shred it finely. Heat the cream, coconut milk, vanilla seeds, lemongrass, and sugar in a saucepan but do not let it boil. Meanwhile, cover the gelatine leaves with cold water for 5 minutes, then squeeze out excess water. Remove the cream mixture from the heat, add the softened gelatine and stir until dissolved. Allow to cool, stirring occasionally, then strain into individual tumbler-style glasses and place in the fridge overnight.

For the passionfruit-chile syrup, scrape the juice and seeds from the passion fruit into a small saucepan, add the stock syrup and heat gently. Leave for 10-15 minutes to infuse, then strain. Add the lime juice and rind and the diced chile and leave to cool.

Arrange the exotic fruits on top of the pannacotta, pour over a little of the chile syrup and serve.

TIP

To make stock syrup, put 1 cup superfine sugar in a saucepan with $1^1/_4$ cups of water and bring slowly to a boil, stirring until the sugar has dissolved. Boil rapidly for 2 minutes to form a light syrup. Leave to cool, then store in a cool place. Use for sweet sauces, ice creams, sorbets etc.

Nutritional value per serving:

Calories: 580

Fats: 48g

Carbohydrates: 35g

Salt: 0.43g

iced coconut parfait with papaya & lime

9 egg yolks

$^2/_3$ cup superfine sugar

9 tablespoons coconut powder

1 cup heavy cream

1 cup Greek yogurt

2 papaya

rind and juice of 2 limes

Line a 2 pint terrine pan with plastic wrap and place it in the freezer. Mix the egg yolks and sugar in a large bowl and cook as shown below. Whisk in the coconut powder. Continue whisking for 10-15 minutes until thick and doubled in volume. Remove the bowl from the heat and continue whisking until the mixture is cold. Whip the cream to the same consistency as the yogurt and lightly fold into the egg mixture with the yogurt. Pour into the prepared pan and freeze for several hours or overnight until firm.

Peel the papaya, cut in half and remove the seeds. Cut the flesh into even slices, shred over the lime rind and squeeze over the juice. Leave to macerate for 30 minutes. Turn out the parfait, remove the plastic wrap and serve in slices accompanied by the fruit.

How to cook using a double boiler

Half fill a saucepan with water and bring to simmering point. Use a Pyrex bowl which fits snugly into the saucepan just above the level of the water.

Nutritional value per serving:

Calories: 397

Fats: 29g

Carbohydrates: 28g

Salt: 0.12g

preserved clementines

1$^1/_4$ cups superfine sugar

6 star anise

8 cloves

2 cinnamon sticks, broken into 2in lengths

6 tablespoons gin

4lb clementines, peeled

In a saucepan, combine the sugar and spices with 2$^3/_4$ cups of water, cover and bring to a boil. Stir to ensure all the sugar is dissolved, stir in the gin, and then set aside to cool.

Pack the clementines loosely into two 1$^3/_4$ pint sterilised jars, distributing the spices as evenly as possible, then pour over the syrup. Leave about $^1/_2$in of space at the top of each jar and seal.

Place the jars in a large saucepan and fill with cold water to come almost, but not quite, to the full height of the jars, leaving about $^3/_4$in. Cover and slowly bring to a boil. Reduce the heat and simmer for about 25 minutes. Remove from the pan and allow to cool.

Store the preserved clementines for up to 5 months.

TIP

Serve on their own, or with cream or ice cream.

Nutritional value per serving:

Calories: 219

Fats: 0g

Carbohydrates: 49g

Salt: 0.02g

pistachio and rosewater ice cream

$^1/_2$ cup superfine sugar

4 egg yolks

$1^1/_2$ cups full-fat milk

$^3/_4$ cup cream for whipping

pinch of saffron threads, soaked in a
   spoonful or two of water

2 tablespoons coarsely chopped pistachios

2 dessertspoons rosewater

In a large heatproof mixing bowl, combine the sugar and egg yolks, and whisk until pale. Bring the milk up to boiling point in a saucepan, remove from the heat and pour on to the egg and sugar mixture, whisking all the time. Pour into a clean saucepan, place over a moderate heat and stir, making sure the mixture doesn't catch (particularly at the edges) until thick. As soon as a line drawn with your finger through the custard on the back of a spoon remains, remove from the heat and pour into a clean bowl. Combine the custard with the cream, and stir in the saffron and the soaking liquid, with the pistachios and rosewater. Transfer to an ice-cream maker and churn until frozen. Remove from the freezer 10-15 minutes before serving.

How to check the custard mixture

If a line drawn with your finger through the mixture on the back of a spoon remains, it is ready. If it overcooks you will end up with sweet scrambled eggs. If you are nervous, pour the mixture through a strainer, which will help to catch the overcooked lumps.

Nutritional value per serving:

Calories: 441

Fats: 32g

Carbohydrates: 33g

Salt: 0.21g

the snake

1 cup whole almonds

3¹/₄ cups ground almonds

¹/₂ cup confectioners' sugar

¹/₂ cup superfine sugar

¹/₂ stick unsalted butter, softened

1 teaspoon unsalted butter

1 teaspoon ground cinnamon

2 teaspoons orange flower water (you could
　also use rosewater)

phyllo pastry

1 egg yolk

Fry the whole almonds in a knob of the butter until golden brown on both sides – take care they do not burn. Either process them or pound them in a pestle and mortar until you have a slightly crunchy texture. Mix into the ground almonds and add the two sugars, the stick of butter, the cinnamon, and orange flower water. With your hands form to a smooth paste and chill for 30 minutes. Preheat the oven to 350°F.

Take two sheets of phyllo pastry and glue them together end to end with a little of the egg yolk. Roll out the almond paste to a tube the thickness of your thumb and lay it the length of the phyllo pastry. Roll the pastry up so that you have a long tube. Repeat this process until all the almond paste is used.

Fashion one of the tubes of filled pastry into a coil, starting from the center. Use egg yolk to stick the ends of pastry together and repeat with the remaining rolls until you have a large coil or 'snake.' Place on a buttered baking sheet. Melt the remaining butter and brush this over the surface of the pastry. Bake in the preheated oven for 25 to 30 minutes, until lightly browned. Leave to cool before serving.

Nutritional value per serving:

Calories: 429

Fats: 33g

Carbohydrates: 24g

Salt: 0.16g

How to make the snake

The snake is constructed by making several small rolls and joining them together in a spriral shape.

pineapple bugles

4 baby pineapples

1 x 4oz packet desiccated coconut

3/4 cup sugar

2 vanilla pods

1in piece of fresh gingerroot, finely chopped

1 red chile, pitted, and finely chopped

juice of 2 limes

4 tablespoons rum

Peel the skins off the pineapples as shown below, leaving the leaves at the top. Pour out the coconut on to a large plate or tray and place to one side.

In a saucepan, mix the sugar, seeds from the vanilla pods, ginger, chile, and the lime juice. Bring to a boil and allow to simmer until the sugar is golden in color.

Dry the pineapples with a clean kitchen paper towel. Pour the hot sugar syrup into a tray and roll the pineapples one by one first in the sugar syrup and then in the coconut. Allow to set. To serve, place on a plate covered with crushed ice, pour over the rum and ignite.

TIP

To judge whether or not a pineapple is ripe, tug at one of the inner leaves – it will come away easily if the pineapple is in the right condition.

How to peel a pineapple

Stand the pineapple upright and cut off the skin in slices. With a sharp knife, cut out the 'eyes' by following the diagonal lines they form round the pineapple.

Nutritional value per serving:

Calories: 409

Fats: 16g

Carbohydrates: 60g

Salt: 0.03g

panna 'ri-cotta'

4 tablespoons milk

²/₃ cup heavy cream

¹/₂ cup superfine sugar

rind of half an orange

¹/₃ cup freshly made strong coffee,
    preferably espresso

half a vanilla pod, split

2 gelatine leaves

2 tablespoons rum

7oz firm ricotta, strained

sprigs of fresh mint, to decorate (optional)

Apricot compote

¹/₂ cup superfine sugar

6 tablespoons water

juice of half a lemon

5-6 medium fresh apricots, pitted and sliced

Put the milk, cream, sugar and orange zest in a saucepan and bring to a boil. Stir in the coffee and scrape in the seeds from the vanilla pod, then add the pod as well. Remove from the heat and allow to cool. Meanwhile, put the gelatine in a small saucepan, cover with cold water and allow to soak for 5 minutes. Heat gently until the gelatine has dissolved.

Take the vanilla pod out of the pan and stir in the rum, sieved ricotta, and the gelatine. Strain through a fine strainer, then pour into 4 ramekins or similar molds and chill for at least 2 hours, until set.

For the compote, put the sugar, water, and lemon juice in a saucepan and bring slowly to a boil, stirring to dissolve the sugar. Reduce the heat, add the sliced apricots and poach for about 5 minutes, until just tender. Remove from the heat and leave to cool, then chill.

Turn out the coffee ricotta custards, or serve them in the ramekins if you prefer, accompanied by the apricot compote and decorated with sprigs of mint, if liked.

Nutritional value per serving:

Calories: 449

Fats: 24g

Carbohydrates: 48g

Salt: 0.22g

rhubarb in chilled syrup with cheese sorbet

1½ cups red wine

4 tablespoons grenadine syrup

juice and rind of 1 orange

1 cinnamon stick

6 tablespoons superfine sugar

1lb 10oz rhubarb, peeled and cut into
   2in lengths

Cheese sorbet

2 cups milk

½ cup superfine sugar

juice and rind of 1 small orange

½ cup cream cheese

For the sorbet, put the milk, sugar, orange juice, and rind in a pan and bring to a boil, stirring to dissolve the sugar, then remove from the heat and leave to cool. Stir this mixture into the cream cheese. Pour into an ice-cream maker and freeze until firm, following the manufacturer's instructions.

If you don't have an ice-cream maker, pour the mixture into a shallow container and put it in the freezer. After about 30 minutes, when the mixture is beginning to set, remove from the freezer and beat well with an electric beater or hand whisk to disperse any ice crystals, then return it to the freezer. Repeat this 2 or 3 times and then freeze until firm.

For the punch syrup, put the wine, grenadine syrup, orange juice and rind, cinnamon, and sugar into a saucepan and boil until reduced by half its volume.

Add the rhubarb to the syrup and cook gently for up to 5 minutes, until the rhubarb is tender and sweet but still holds its shape. Transfer to a bowl and allow to cool, then chill thoroughly. Serve with scoops of the cheese sorbet.

Nutritional value per serving:

Calories: 623

Fats: 23g

Carbohydrates: 88g

Salt: 0.68g

TIP

For an interesting contrast, you could serve the rhubarb and punch syrup with the sorbet while they are still warm.

warming
winter
desserts

tamarind-baked winter fruits

1 vanilla pod, split open lengthways

1 cup palm sugar (or demerara sugar)

2 lemongrass stalks, outer layers removed,
    tender inner core finely shredded

1$\frac{1}{2}$ teaspoons finely shredded fresh gingerroot

4 star anise

2 tablespoons tamarind paste

$\frac{1}{2}$ stick unsalted butter

2 ripe pears, peeled, cored, and quartered

6 ripe plums, halved and pitted

8 prunes, pitted

8 dried figs

12 dried apricots

$\frac{1}{3}$ cup sweet white wine

juice of 1 lime

Preheat the oven to 375°F. Combine the vanilla pod, sugar, lemongrass, gingerroot, star anise, and tamarind in a pan with $\frac{2}{3}$ cup of water, bring to a boil and simmer for 10 minutes. Remove from the heat and set aside.

Heat a casserole or deep, flameproof baking dish on the stove, add the butter, then add all the fruit and fry for 1-2 minutes, until lightly caramelized. Pour over the wine, lime juice and tamarind mixture and stir to coat the fruit. Place in the oven for 10-12 minutes, until the fruit is tender and lightly glazed. Serve warm.

Nutritional value per serving:

Calories: 515

Fats: 11g

Carbohydrates: 100g

Salt: 0.13g

grilled figs in cilantro-lime syrup

1 bunch of cilantro, leaves and stalks separated

juice from a 2in piece of fresh
gingerroot (see below)

juice and shredded rind of 2 limes

1¼ cups Sauternes (or other sweet wine)

⅔ cup glucose syrup

4 green cardamom pods, split

12 ripe purple figs

1½ teaspoons vanilla sugar

Put the cilantro stalks in a pan with the ginger juice, lime juice and rind, wine, glucose syrup and cardamom pods and bring gently to a boil. Reduce the heat and simmer for 5 minutes. Add the whole figs and poach gently for 3 minutes, then remove from the heat and leave to cool. Remove the figs from the syrup and set aside. Return the syrup to the heat and simmer until it begins to thicken. Meanwhile, blanch the cilantro leaves in boiling water for a few seconds, then drain well and refresh in iced water. Drain and pat dry. Add the leaves to the hot syrup and leave for 2-3 minutes. Pour the mixture into a blender and blitz until smooth. Strain and leave to cool, then chill.

Cut the figs lengthways in half and place on a baking sheet. Sprinkle with the vanilla sugar and place under a hot broiler for 2-3 minutes, until caramelized. Arrange the figs on serving plates, drizzle over the syrup and serve.

How to make ginger juice

For natural ginger juice, shred a piece of gingerroot and squeeze through cheesecloth. When shredding you will find that the tougher fibers get caught in the shredder; discard these.

Nutritional value per serving:

Calories: 264

Fats: 1g

Carbohydrates: 52g

Salt: 0.37g

caramelized **banana** tart

Base

6 tablespoons butter

3 tablespoons soft brown (Barbados) sugar

3 tablespoons superfine sugar

4-5 bananas

a little freshly squeezed lemon juice

Topping

1 ripe banana, mashed

2 tablespoons sour cream

1 teaspoon pure vanilla essence

1 cup superfine sugar

6 tablespoons butter

2 eggs

1½ cups self-raising flour

Preheat the oven to 350°F.

Melt the butter in a large flameproof and ovenproof sauté pan, add the sugars and stir well to dissolve. Slice the bananas and arrange in concentric circles over the base. Squeeze a little freshly squeezed lemon juice over the bananas.

Next make the topping. Mash the banana, add the sour cream and vanilla essence. Cream the butter, add the superfine sugar and beat until light and fluffy. Add the eggs one at a time and continue to beat well. Gently fold in the flour and banana mixture alternately.

Spread the topping evenly and carefully over the bananas. Bake in the pre-heated oven for 45-50 minutes or until golden brown and fully cooked. Allow to rest in the dish for 5-10 minutes before turning out onto a warm serving plate so that the bananas are uppermost. Be careful of the hot juices.

Serve warm with softly whipped cream or sour cream.

Nutritional value per serving:

Calories: 578

Fats: 24 g

Carbohydrates: 89g

Salt: 0.83g

saffron pavlova with lime curd

6 egg whites

1 cup superfine sugar

4 pinches saffron powder

1 teaspoon white wine vinegar

1 teaspoon boiling water

1/2 teaspoon vanilla extract

1 tablespoon cornstarch

heavy cream or plain yogurt, to serve

a little blanched shredded lime rind,
   to decorate

Lime curd

6 egg yolks

1 cup superfine sugar

juice and shredded rind 6 large limes
   (you will need 2/3 cup juice)

pinch of salt

1 stick chilled unsalted butter, diced

Preheat the oven to 250°F. Put the egg whites and sugar in a clean, dry bowl and whisk until they form stiff peaks. Mix the saffron powder with the vinegar and boiling water, then whisk it into the beaten whites with the vanilla extract. Finally fold in the cornstarch.

Line 2 baking sheets with baking parchment and spread the meringue mixture on it in 6 mounded circles (alternatively, pipe the mixture into 6 nests, using a piping bag with a plain nozzle). Bake for 50-60 minutes, until they are crisp but still pale on the outside and have a soft marshmallow center. Store in an airtight container until needed.

For the lime curd, beat the egg yolks and sugar together until thick and creamy, then add the lime juice and rind. Place in a heavy saucepan and cook, stirring, over a low heat until the mixture thickens a little. Add the salt and immediately remove from the heat. Whisk in the chilled diced butter and leave to cool. Cover and keep in the fridge until required.

To serve, top each saffron pavlova with a good dollop of lime curd and then pour over some cream or yogurt and decorate with a little blanched lime rind.

Nutritional value per serving: ·

Calories: 585

Fats: 32g

Carbohydrates: 69g

Salt: 0.42g

crêpes suzette

Batter

makes 8 pancakes

1/2 cup all-purpose flour

1 tablespoon oil

1 egg

1 egg yolk

2 teaspoons orange curaçao liqueur

2/3 cup milk

Sauce

shredded rind of 2 large ripe oranges

6 tablespoons softened butter

4 tyablespoons superfine sugar

generous tablespoon each of brandy
   and curaçao

First make the batter: put the flour in a bowl and make a well in the center. Into this pour the oil, egg, egg yolk, and orange curaçao. Stir, gradually drawing in the flour from the sides. Add the milk slowly until it is the consistency of thin cream. Set aside in the refrigerator for 30 minutes. Then make the crêpes by putting a small ladleful of batter at a time into a hot non-stick skillet or pancake pan; as soon as bubbles rise to the surface, flip over and cook the other side. Keep the crêpes ready for use later.

For the sauce, add the rind of the oranges to the butter and sugar, and cream vigorously until smooth.

To finish: put the pan over a high heat. Melt about 1 tablespoon butter in it. When bubbling, put a cooked crêpe in and heat through, turning so that both sides get warm. Fold it into a fan shape and rest it against the side of the pan. Continue in the same way with the remaining pancakes. There should be enough to make 8 pancakes altogether. Sprinkle them with superfine sugar. Pour over brandy and curaçao. Set alight, to burn off the alcohol, keeping your face away from the flames. Tilt the pan and spoon the juices over the pancakes until the flame subsides. Serve immediately on hot plates.

TIP

When cooked, crêpes may be stacked on top of each other and peeled apart later. Crêpes stored in this way may be kept in the fridge and used hours or even days later. They will peel off each other easily.

Nutritional value per serving:

Calories: 147

Fats: 6g

Carbohydrates: 16g

Salt: 0.06g

roasted pears in ginger butter

2 tablespoons sugar

2 tablespoons honey

1in piece of fresh gingerroot, finely shredded

4 tablespoons white wine

1in piece of cinnamon stick

4 ripe but firm pears, preferably Williams

1/2 stick unsalted butter

2 tablespoons rum

1 teaspoon finely chopped preserved
   stem ginger

Put the sugar, honey, shredded gingerroot, wine, cinnamon, and 2/3 cup of water in a saucepan and bring to a boil, stirring. Simmer until the syrup has reduced by half, then strain and set aside.

Peel and core the pears and cut them in half vertically, but leave the stalks on. Heat a large skillet (big enough to take the 8 pear halves lying flat), add the butter, and heat until it begins to foam. Add the pears, laying them flat around the pan, core-side down. Cook for 2-3 minutes, until golden underneath, then turn and cook the other side. Add the strained syrup and the rum to the pan and cover with a lid. Reduce the heat and leave the pears to caramelize in the buttery syrup, turning occasionally – this will take 4-5 minutes.

Arrange the pears on serving plates, add the preserved ginger to the syrup and pour it over the pears.

Nutritional value per serving:

Calories: 207

Fats: 10g

Carbohydrates: 23g

Salt: 0.01g

blue cheese and pecan pie

Pastry

3 cups all-purpose flour

2 sticks unsalted butter, cut into small pieces

pinch of salt

1 cup confectioners' sugar

finely shredded rind of half a lemon

1 egg beaten

5 tablespoons unsalted butter

4 tablespoons golden syrup

1½ cups mild blue cheese, cut into small cubes

¾ cup soft brown sugar

3 eggs

2 tablespoons rum

½ teaspoon vanilla extract

pinch of salt

1¼ cups pecan nuts

Nutritional value per serving:

Calories: 1557

Fats: 100g

Carbohydrates: 147g

Salt: 1.64g

Preheat the oven to 375°F. Sift the flour onto a work surface and make a well in the center. Put the butter, salt, sugar, and lemon rind in the well and add the egg. With your fingertips, gradually bring the flour into the center until all the ingredients form a soft dough. Knead lightly for 1 minute, until smooth, then form into a ball. Wrap in plastic wrap and chill for 2 hours. Roll out the pastry on a floured surface to ⅛in thick and use to line a 9in flan pan, 1in deep. Bake blind for 10 minutes, then remove the paper and beans and bake for a further 5 minutes. Remove from the oven and reduce the temperature to 350°F.

Heat the butter and golden syrup in a saucepan, add half the cheese and stir until melted. In a bowl, whisk together the sugar, eggs, rum, vanilla, and salt. Add the pecan nuts and then stir into the syrup and cheese mixture. Add the remaining cheese and pour the mixture into the pastry case. Bake for about 30 minutes, until just set.

How to bake blind

Cut a circle of silicone paper and place over the pastry case. Fill with ceramic beans, as here, or use dried beans such as navy or kidney beans, or even rice.

date crumble slice

1 stick butter, softened
4 tablespoons demerara sugar
1 egg yolk
$1/2$ cup ground almonds
$13/4$ cups all-purpose flour
$12/3$ cups chopped dates
$1/2$ cup cream cheese
1 teaspoon mixed spice
1 tablespoon raw brown sugar
confectioners' sugar, to dust
light cream or custard, to serve

Preheat the oven to 350°F.

Prepare the dough. In a large bowl, or the bowl of a food processor, cream together the butter and sugar, add the egg yolk and beat well. Fold in the ground almonds and flour. It may be necessary to work the mixture with your hands at this stage. It will look very dry but do not be tempted to add any liquid. After a short while it will easily come together into a ball. Wrap in plastic wrap and chill until the dough is very firm. This will take 1-2 hours.

Place the chopped dates in a saucepan and cover with water. Bring to a boil and cook for 3 minutes. Turn off the heat and allow to stand for 5 minutes or until the dates are soft. Drain well.

Remove the dough from the refrigerator and cut in two. Using a coarse shredder, shred half of the dough to cover the base of a 13 x 4in rectangular or 9in round pie pan. Press it down loosely. When cooked it will melt to form a base. Cover with an even layer of the dates. Spoon the cream cheese over the fruit and spread to cover. Shred the remaining dough over the top. Mix the spice and extra sugar together, then sprinkle onto the pie. Bake for 35-40 minutes until golden brown.

Remove from the pan and dust with confectioners' sugar before serving with light cream or custard.

Nutritional value per serving:
Calories: 433
Fats: 25g
Carbohydrates: 50g
Salt: 0.44g

parkin

1 cup all-purpose flour

2 cups medium oatmeal

2 tablespoons brown sugar

1in piece of fresh root gingerroot,
   finely shredded

pinch of ground ginger

pinch of salt

1 cup golden syrup

7 tablespoons unsalted butter

1 teaspoon baking soda

4 tablespoons full-fat milk, warmed

Preheat the oven to 325°F. Mix all the dry ingredients together in a large bowl. Place the syrup and butter in a saucepan and heat gently until the butter has melted. Dissolve the baking soda in the warm milk, then pour both liquids into the flour mixture and stir well.

Pour into an oiled and lined 8in square cake pan and bake for 45-50 minutes; when it is done, a cocktail stick inserted in the center should come out clean. Leave to cool in the pan, then turn out and cut into squares.

TIP

Store parkin in an airtight container; the longer you keep it, the stickier and better it will become.

Nutritional value per serving:

Calories: 449

Fats: 17g

Carbohydrates: 72g

Salt:1.22 g

vanilla & orange marmalade pudding

3/4 cup superfine sugar

5/8 cup unsalted butter

1 teaspoon vanilla extract

3 eggs, separated

1 cup self-raising flour, sifted

4 tablespoons golden syrup

4 tablespoons good-quality orange marmalade

2 vanilla pods

Preheat the oven to 375°F. In a bowl, beat 1/2 cup of the sugar with the butter until pale and creamy. Add the vanilla extract, then beat in the egg yolks one at a time. Fold in the flour. In a separate bowl, whisk the egg whites with the remaining sugar until they form stiff peaks. Stir a quarter of the whites into the egg yolk mixture to loosen it, then carefully fold in the rest.

Gently heat the golden syrup and marmalade together in a saucepan. Slit the vanilla pods open lengthways and scrape out the seeds with a small teaspoon or the point of a sharp knife. Add to the marmalade and syrup and mix well.

Oil eight ramekins and place 2 tablespoons of the vanilla marmalade in the base of each one. Top with the pudding mixture, filling them three-quarters full, and tap the ramekins to release any air pockets. Cover with aluminum foil and place in a roasting pan of hot water (the water should come halfway up the side of the ramekins). Place in the oven and bake for 40–45 minutes.

Run a knife around the edge of each pudding and turn out on to a serving plate. Serve with copious amounts of cream.

Nutritional value per serving:

Calories: 325

Fats: 18g

Carbohydrates: 41g

Salt: 0.25g

tunisian **orange** cake

3/4 cup slightly stale white breadcrumbs

1 cup superfine sugar

1 cup ground almonds

1 1/2 level teaspoons baking powder

3/4 cup sunflower oil

4 eggs

rind of 1 large unwaxed orange, finely shredded

rind of 1/2 unwaxed lemon, finely shredded

cream, Greek yogurt or sour cream, to serve

Citrus syrup

juice of 1 unwaxed orange

juice of 1/2 unwaxed lemon

1/3 cup sugar

2 cloves

1 cinnamon stick

Line the base of an 8in round pan with a round of waxed paper. Oil and flour the pan. Mix the breadcrumbs with the sugar, almonds and baking powder. Whisk the oil with the eggs, pour into the dry ingredients and mix well. Add the orange and lemon rinds. Pour the mixture into the prepared pan. Put into a cold oven, and turn on with the heat set to 350°F.

Bake for 45-60 minutes or until the cake is golden brown. A skewer inserted into the center should come out clean. Allow to cool for 5 minutes before turning out onto a plate.

Meanwhile make the citrus syrup. Put all the ingredients into a stainless-steel saucepan, bring gently to a boil, stirring until the sugar has dissolved completely. Simmer for 3 minutes. While the cake is still warm, pierce it with a skewer. Spoon the hot syrup over the cake. Allow to cool.

Spoon excess syrup back over the cake every now and then until it is all soaked up. You can remove the cloves and cinnamon stick or leave them on top of the cake for decoration. Serve with softly whipped cream or thick Greek yogurt.

Nutritional value per serving:

Calories: 640

Fats: 43g

Carbohydrates: 57g

Salt: 0.67g

coconut cassava cake

3lb cassava, peeled and shredded

1 large fresh coconut, shredded

1lb white cheese (Cheddar is fine), shredded

pinch of salt

2 egg yolks

1 cup milk

1 cup sugar

4 tablespoons softened butter

1 teaspoon aniseeds, lightly toasted
   and crushed

Place the cassava, the coconut, and the cheese in a bowl. Add the remaining ingredients and mix together to make a smooth soft dough. Set it aside for an hour to swell.

Preheat the oven to 300°F.

Transfer the dough to a buttered baking pan – a large loaf pan is perfect – and bake for an hour, until firm to the finger, well-risen and browned. Surprisingly light and moist – it is delicious with fresh pineapple.

Nutritional value per serving:

Calories: 836

Fats: 46g

Carbohydrates: 93g

Salt: 1.45g

plum pudding

6oz shredded beef suet (or use the vegetarian
   substitute)

$3/4$ cup sugar

3 cups soft breadcrumbs

$1^1/3$ cups currants

$1^1/3$ cups raisins

$1/2$ cup candied peel

1-2 teaspoons mixed spice

pinch of salt

2 tablespoons flour

3 eggs

3 tablespoons flesh of a baked apple

3 tablespoons Irish whiskey

Brandy butter

6 tablespoons butter

$3/4$ cup confectioners' sugar

2-6 tablespoons brandy

Mix the dry ingredients thoroughly. Whisk the eggs and add them with the apple and whiskey. Stir very well indeed. Fill a pudding bowl. Cover with a round of waxed paper or a butter-paper pressed down on top of the pudding. Put a large round of waxed or brown paper over the top of a 3 pint pudding bowl, tying it firmly under the rim. Place in a saucepan one-third full of boiling water and simmer for 10 hours. Do not allow the water to boil over the top and do not let it boil dry either. Store in a cool place until needed.

To make the brandy butter, cream the butter until very light, add the icing sugar and beat again. Then beat in the brandy, drop by drop. If you have a food processor, use it: you will get a wonderfully light and fluffy butter.

On Christmas Day: Boil for $1^1/2$-2 hours before serving. Serve with brandy butter.

TIP
Leftover pudding may be fried in butter.

Nutritional value per serving:

Calories: 712

Fats: 30g

Carbohydrates: 105g

Salt: 1.02g

treacle **pear** pudding

2 tablespoons butter

2 heaped tablespoons golden syrup

1 pear

⅝ cup butter, softened

¾ cup superfine sugar

2 eggs, beaten

1¼ cups self-raising flour

3 tablespoons cider

light cream, to serve

Use a little of the butter to oil a 12 pint pudding bowl. Spoon the golden syrup into the base of the bowl. Peel, core, and dice the pear and place on top of the syrup. Dot with the remaining butter.

Cream the butter and sugar until light and fluffy. Incorporate the eggs little by little, beating well between each addition. Sift the flour and fold in, adding enough cider to give a firm dropping consistency. Spoon the mixture into the pudding bowl on top of the fruit. Cover with a disc of buttered waxed paper. Cut a circle of aluminum foil that will overhang the top of the basin by 3in. Make a ½ in pleat in the foil then place it over the bowl and tie securely with string. The pleat allows for expansion during cooking.

Stand the bowl on a trivet in a deep saucepan. Add enough water to come 2in up the sides of the bowl. Cover with a tightly fitting lid and steam for 1-1½ hours. To test if the pudding is cooked, remove the aluminum foil and waxed paper disc and insert a small skewer into the center; it should come out clean. If not cooked, re-cover the bowl and steam for a little longer. If cooked ahead of time, turn off the heat and leave until required.

Lift the pudding from the pan, snip the string and remove the aluminum foil and the waxed paper disc. Invert the bowl onto a serving dish. Serve with light cream or cinnamon custard.

TIP

If you prefer the topping of your pudding to be sticky rather than syrupy, add a couple of tablespoons of fresh breadcrumbs on top of the golden syrup before adding the fruit. This absorbs some of the liquid and gives a more traditional treacle pudding texture.

Nutritional value per serving:

Calories: 468

Fats: 26g

Carbohydrates: 57g

Salt: 0.93g

pumpkin and ricotta torte with pinenuts

1lb slice of pumpkin, pitted and sliced into
   wedges

3 tablespoons water

11oz sweet shortcrust pastry

1lb 2oz ricotta cheese

6 tablespoons sour cream

3 eggs

1 cup superfine sugar

1 rounded tablespoon flour

½ cup pinenuts

icing sugar, to dust

Preheat the oven to 350°F. Place the pumpkin wedges in a roasting pan with 3 tablespoons of water, cover with a sheet of aluminum foil and bake for 1-1½ hours until completely tender. Cool, then remove the skin and process the flesh in a food processor until smooth.

Oil the sides of a 8½in springform pan. This will help to hold the pastry in place. Use three-quarters of the pastry to line the prepared pan, pressing the dough well into the base and sides. Chill. Roll the remaining pastry to form a rectangle and cut into long strips about ½in wide. Lay on a baking sheet and chill while preparing the filling.

In a large bowl beat together the ricotta cheese and the pumpkin purée until smooth. Stir in the sour cream. Beat the eggs, then add to the purée mixture with the caster sugar and flour. Blend well together. Pour or spoon into the pastry case and sprinkle the pinenuts over the top.

Brush the pastry edge with a little water or egg white, then lay the chilled strips of pastry over the torte in a lattice pattern. Trim off the ends and bake for 45-55 minutes. The filling will rise and the crust will have a gorgeous golden color. Switch off the oven and allow the torte to cool inside.

Remove from the pan and dust with confectioners' sugar.

Nutritional value per serving:

Calories: 473

Fats: 26g

Carbohydrates: 50g

Salt: 0.39g

rhubarb crumble with vanilla cream

4 cups all-purpose flour, sifted

pinch of salt

2 sticks unsalted butter, cut into cubes

1 cup superfine sugar

3lb fresh rhubarb

1¼ cups superfine sugar

finely shredded rind and juice of 2 medium-
sized oranges

Vanilla cream

2½ cups heavy cream

¼ cup icing sugar

1 vanilla pod, split lengthways, pitted

Preheat the oven to 375°F.

In an electric mixer, add the flour, salt, butter, and cup of sugar. Mix until the texture resembles fine breadcrumbs.

Wash the rhubarb, and trim top and bottom. Cut the rhubarb into 2in long pieces. Mix with the 1¼ cups sugar, orange rind and juice, then place in an ovenproof dish. Cover the dish with aluminum foil, and bake for 30 minutes until the rhubarb is soft but still retains its shape.

Turn down the oven to 330°F.

Divide the rhubarb and the crumble topping between the serving dishes you are using. Bake for about 30 minutes, until you start to see the liquid bubbling out and the crumble is golden brown. While it cooks, prepare the cream.

Place the chilled cream in a mixing bowl, then add the confectioners' sugar and vanilla. Whisk, by hand or with an electric mixer, until the mixture begins to thicken. If using an electric mixer, do not leave unattended, otherwise you could over-beat the cream and turn it into butter. The vanilla cream is best served as soon as it is made, which takes only a few minutes.

Nutritional value per serving:

Calories: 803

Fats: 48g

Carbohydrates: 92g

Salt: 0.28g

wicked &
wonderful

hazelnut praline

2/3 cup light cream

2/3 cup white chocolate

2/3 cup hazelnut nougat (available in
   specialist shops)

2 teaspoons pâté noisette (available in
   specialist shops)

1 gelatine leaf, soaked in a small amount of
   water

1 cup whipping cream, lightly whipped

ice cream and chocolate curls or sticks,
   to serve

finely chopped hazelnuts, to serve

Put the cream in a saucepan and bring to a boil. Boil for 1-2 minutes, then add the white chocolate. When it starts to melt mix in the nougat and pâté noisette. Take off the heat and allow to cool slightly, then add the gelatine as the mixture starts to cool down.

Fold in the whipped cream. Pour into dariole molds and freeze until set. To remove from the molds, dip the base in boiling water for 10 seconds and then invert on to a plate. Serve with vanilla, chocolate or white chocolate ice-cream and chocolate curls or sticks. Sprinkle with finely chopped hazelnuts.

Nutritional value per serving:

Calories: 587

Fats: 47g

Carbohydrates: 37g

Salt: 0.25g

SERVES 6

PREPARATION TIME: 10 MINUTES

COOKING TIME: 40 MINUTES

CHILLING TIME: 3-5 HOURS

hot chocolate fondants

2½ sticks unsalted butter, plus extra for oiling

3 tablespoons cocoa powder, plus extra for dusting

9oz dark chocolate (70 percent cocoa solids)

1 cup all-purpose flour

2 eggs

1 cup superfine sugar

Oil 6 x 7fl oz dariole molds with a little butter and then dust with cocoa powder. Set aside. Break the chocolate into pieces and place in a large heatproof bowl set over a saucepan of simmering water. Allow to melt and then gradually whisk in the butter. Set aside and allow to cool a little.

Sift the flour and cocoa powder into a bowl. Whisk the eggs and sugar in another bowl until pale and fluffy, then fold into the cooled chocolate mixture until well combined. Finally fold in the flour mixture and either pipe or spoon into the prepared dariole molds until each one is no more than three-quarters full, gently tapping to remove any air bubbles. Cover with plastic wrap and chill for at least 3 hours or up to 5 hours.

Preheat the oven to 400°F. Arrange the dariole molds on a baking sheet and bake for 12-14 minutes. Allow to rest for a minute or two, then invert each dariole mold into the middle of a wide-rimmed bowl and serve immediately with a spoonful of whipped cream and some warmed chocolate sauce, if liked.

TIP

These chocolate fondants can be made well in advance, as they improve if they have been allowed to rest for at least three hours before baking.

Nutritional value per serving:

Calories: 487

Fats: 57g

Carbohydrates: 67g

Salt: 0.21g

bitter **chocolate sorbet** with raspberries

$3/4$ cup superfine sugar

$1^1/_2$oz liquid glucose

$1/3$ cup milk

3 tablespoons cocoa powder (good quality)

$3^1/_2$oz dark chocolate (70 percent cocoa solids), finely chopped

2 cups fresh raspberries

Place the sugar in a heavy saucepan with $1^3/_4$ cups of water, the liquid glucose, milk, and cocoa powder. Bring to a boil, stirring from time to time, then simmer for 2 minutes, whisking constantly to prevent the bottom of the pan from catching.

Remove the pan from the heat and add the chocolate, stirring until the chocolate has melted. Pass through a fine strainer into a jug, cover with plastic wrap and chill for a few hours until it is really cold.

Now you can either churn the mixture in an ice-cream machine or pour it into a plastic container and freeze until it is almost firm. If doing the latter, scrape the mixture into a food processor and whizz until smooth. Pour it back into the plastic container and repeat one more time. Return the sorbet to the freezer and freeze until firm.

To serve, quickly dip two tablespoons into boiling water and use to shape the sorbet into quenelles. Arrange three in each wide rimmed serving bowl and decorate with the raspberries. Serve immediately.

Nutritional value per serving:

Calories: 372

Fats: 13g

Carbohydrates: 63g

Salt: 0.32g

SERVES 4-6

PREPARATION TIME: 15 MINUTES

COOKING TIME: 45 MINUTES

FREEZING TIME: 1-3 HOURS

white chocolate & basil profiteroles with hot dark chocolate sauce

White chocolate and basil ice cream

10 basil leaves, leaves and stalks separated

$3/4$ cup heavy cream

$3/4$ cup full-fat milk

7oz white chocolate, broken into pieces

4 egg yolks

2 tablespoons superfine sugar

Choux pastry

$3/4$ cup full-fat milk

5 tablespoons unsalted butter, diced

$1^1/2$ tablespoons superfine sugar

1 heaped cup all-purpose flour

4 eggs

1 egg yolk, beaten with 2 tablespoons milk

2 tablespoons slivered almonds

Chocolate sauce

$3^1/2$ oz good-quality dark chocolate

$1/2$ tablespoon superfine sugar

6 tablespoons heavy cream

small knob of butter

Nutritional value per serving:

Calories: 1237

Fats: 93g

Carbohydrates: 82g

Salt: 0.59g

To make the ice cream, put the basil stalks in a saucepan with the cream and milk, bring gently to a boil and simmer for 1 minute. Add the white chocolate, stir well, then remove from the heat and infuse for 10 minutes. In a bowl, whisk together the egg yolks and sugar until creamy. Strain the basil-infused cream on to the egg yolks, whisking constantly, then return to the pan and cook, stirring, over a low heat, until the mixture thickens (do not let it boil). Remove from the heat and leave to cool. Stir in the torn basil leaves, pour into an ice-cream machine and freeze.

Next make the choux pastry. Preheat the oven to 400°F. Put the milk, butter, and sugar in a saucepan. As soon as it comes to a boil, rain in the flour and beat with a wooden spoon until the mixture leaves the sides of the pan clean. Allow to cool slightly, then beat in the eggs one by one to give a thick, glossy mixture.

Lightly oil a baking sheet and sprinkle it with a little water. Fit a pastry bag with a 1in plain nozzle and pipe out walnut-sized mounds of the choux pastry, brush with a little beaten egg wash and sprinkle over the flaked almonds. Bake for 15 minutes, then open the oven door slightly and leave for a further 10 minutes so that they dry out. Remove from the oven, pierce each profiterole with a skewer so the steam can escape, then allow to cool.

For the chocolate sauce, place all the ingredients in a saucepan and bring gently to a boil, then whisk until smooth, adding a little boiling water if it is too thick. To serve, cut each profiterole in half horizontally, fill with a ball of the ice cream and top with the lid. Arrange on serving plates and pour the hot chocolate sauce over and around.

velvet chocolate mousse with mint glass biscuits

1½ cups heavy cream

1⅓ cups full-fat milk

6 egg yolks

⅔ cups superfine sugar

2 gelatine leaves

13oz good-quality dark chocolate (at least 70 percent cocoa solids), chopped

Mint glass biscuits

2 tablespoons mint leaves, blanched for 10 seconds and dried

1 stick unsalted butter

⅓ cup golden syrup

4 tablespoons crème de menthe

1 cup superfine sugar

1 cup all-purpose flour

Nutritional value per serving:

Calories: 1775

Fats: 106g

Carbohydrates: 190g

Salt: 0.72g

Bring the cream and milk to a boil in a saucepan. In a separate bowl, whisk together the egg yolks and sugar until light and creamy. Whisking constantly, pour in the cream and milk and stir well. Return to the pan and cook, stirring, over a low heat, until the mixture is thick enough to coat the back of the spoon. Remove from the heat. Cover the gelatine leaves with cold water and leave to soak for 5 minutes. Drain well, squeezing out excess water, and add to the custard mixture. Stir well to dissolve the gelatine.

Place the chocolate in a bowl, pour over the hot custard and leave to melt, stirring occasionally. When the chocolate has melted, strain the mixture through a fine strainer into a bowl. Leave to cool, cover with plastic wrap and chill for at least 4 hours, until set.

To make the biscuits, chop the blanched mint leaves finely and set aside. Put the butter, golden syrup, and crème de menthe in a saucepan and heat gently until the butter has melted. Mix the sugar and flour together in a bowl, then pour in the syrup mixture, add the mint and stir well to form a paste. Cover with plastic wrap and chill for 1 hour, until very cold.

Preheat the oven to 350°F. Remove the biscuit mixture from the fridge and shape into 12 balls, 1in in diameter. Place them well spaced out on two baking sheets lined with baking parchment and press each one out to form a small disc. Bake for 8-10 minutes, until pale golden, then remove from the oven and allow to cool and crisp up. Store in a sealed container until ready to use.

To serve, layer the biscuits with the chocolate mousse.

hot **chocolate** mousse

¹/₂ stick butter, melted

¹/₃ cup superfine sugar, for coating

9oz extra-bitter chocolate (70 percent
     cocoa solids)

1 stick butter

8 eggs, separated

1 cup superfine sugar

¹/₂ cup all-purpose flour, sifted

3oz extra-bitter chocolate, chopped into
     small pieces

confectioners' sugar, to dust

1 cup cream for whipping

Nutritional value per serving:

Calories: 463

Fats: 38g

Carbohydrates: 28g

Salt: 0.3g

Preheat the oven to 325°F.

Brush the insides of six small teacups with melted butter and coat with superfine sugar.

Cut the chocolate and butter into 1in pieces, then place in a metal bowl over a saucepan of barely simmering water to melt. Do not allow the chocolate to get too hot as this will make it difficult to combine with the other ingredients. In an electric mixer, whisk the egg whites on a high speed until foamy. Add the superfine sugar gradually, continuing to whisk until the consistency is smooth, glossy, and stiff. Remove the chocolate from the heat, add the egg yolks and mix thoroughly. Fold in the egg whites and add the sifted flour. Continue to fold until all the ingredients are well combined. Remove the cups from the refrigerator. Divide the extra chopped chocolate pieces between them. Spoon the mousse mixture into the cups until each is three-quarters full.

Boil a kettle of water. Put the mousses into a deep roasting pan, then pour boiling water into the pan to halfway up the molds. Cook the mousses for about 20 minutes or until well risen above the edge of the molds.

Carefully remove the tea cups from the water – remembering they will be hot. Place them on a clean dish towel to drain away any excess water. Dust with confectioners' sugar and serve with a spoonful of whipped cream on the side.

lemon tart

4 sticks butter

1 cup sugar

5 cups self-raising flour

2 eggs

Filling

4 cups heavy cream

rind and juice of 7 lemons

3/4 cup sugar

10 egg yolks

Preheat the oven to 325°F.

To make the pastry, combine the butter, sugar, and flour together in a food processor. Add the eggs and mix to make a smooth dough. Wrap the dough in plastic wrap and chill for at least 30 minutes before using.

Roll out the pastry and use to line one 12in oiled flan dish, or 4 individual flan dishes. Transfer to the freezer for 20 minutes. Bake straight from the freezer for 10 minutes, or until golden brown. Remove from the oven and allow to cool. Reduce the oven temperature to 225°F.

To make the filling, bring the cream and lemon rind to a boil in a saucepan. Combine the sugar, egg yolks, and lemon juice in a bowl. Whisk the cream mixture into the egg mixture, combining thoroughly. Strain the filling into the tart shell and bake for 20-30 minutes.

Nutritional value per serving:

Calories: 1210

Fats: 74g

Carbohydrates: 128g

Salt: 1.12g

chocolate **almond** gâteau

4oz best-quality dark chocolate

2 tablespoons red Jamaica rum

1 cup whole almonds

1 stick butter, preferably unsalted

1/2 cup superfine sugar

3 eggs, separated

1 tablespoon superfine sugar

1/2 cup all-purpose white flour

1/2 cup whole almonds or best quality
   ground almonds, blanched and peeled

Chocolate icing

4oz best quality dark chocolate

2 tablespoons red Jamaica rum

1 stick unsalted butter

crystallized violets, to decorate

toasted slivered almonds, to decorate

Nutritional value per serving:

Calories: 607

Fats: 47g

Carbohydrates: 36g

Salt: 0.34g

Preheat the oven to 350°F.

Oil 2 x 7in cake pans and line the base of each with waxed paper. Melt the chocolate with the rum on a very gentle heat. Grind the almonds in a food processor; they should still be slightly gritty.

Cream the butter, and then add the sugar, beating until light and fluffy. Beat in the egg yolks one by one. Whisk the egg whites with a pinch of salt until stiff. Add 1 tablespoon of sugar and continue to whisk until they reach the stiff peak stage. Add the melted chocolate to the butter and sugar mixture and then add the almonds. Fold in a quarter of the egg white mixture followed by a quarter of the sifted flour. Fold in the remaining egg white mixture and flour alternately until they have all been added.

Divide the mixture between the two prepared tins and make a hollow in the center of each cake. Bake in the oven for 19-25 minutes.

IMPORTANT: The cake should be slightly underdone in the center. Sides should be cooked but the center a little unset. Allow to cool for a few minutes in the tins, turn out gently onto a wire rack, remove the paper, and allow to get cold.

For the frosting, melt the chocolate with the rum in a Pyrex bowl over a low heat. Beat in the unsalted butter a tablespoon at a time. Beat occasionally until cool. If the frosting liquefies, put it into the fridge to firm up, then whisk until stiff.

When the cake is completely cold, fill and cover with the mixture. Pipe any remaining frosting around the top and decorate with slivered almonds and crystallized violets.

brownies

2oz best quality dark chocolate

1 stick butter

1 cup superfine sugar

2 eggs, lightly whisked

$^1/_2$ teaspoon vanilla extract

$^3/_4$ cup cake flour

$^1/_2$ teaspoon baking powder

pinch salt

1 cup chopped walnuts

Preheat the oven to 350°F.

Melt the chocolate in a bowl over a saucepan of gently simmering water or in a low oven. Cream the butter and sugar and beat in the eggs, vanilla extract, and melted chocolate. Lastly stir in the flour, baking powder, salt and chopped nuts. Spread the mixture into an 8in square pan and bake in the oven for about 30-35 minutes. Cut into 2in squares for serving.

Nutritional value per serving:

Calories: 185

Fats: 12g

Carbohydrates: 18g

Salt: 0.25g

coffee granita

4 cups freshly made espresso coffee

5 tablespoons sugar

$3/4$ cup cream for whipping

Put the coffee and sugar in a saucepan and gently heat until the sugar has dissolved – you may need more sugar to taste, so check. Remember, too, that because it is to be eaten chilled, the sweetness will be less pronounced.

Pour into a flat plastic container and freeze, stirring every hour, so the crystals don't get too big.

To serve, remove from the freezer about 40 minutes before serving. Break up with a wooden spoon and place in 6-8 iced long-stemmed glasses. Whip the cream, add to the glasses and serve.

Nutritional value per serving:

Calories: 177

Fats: 13g

Carbohydrates: 15g

Salt: 0.04g

chocolate tart with curled
chocolate ganache

1³/₄ cups flour

³/₄ cup superfine sugar

1³/₄ sticks unsalted butter, cubed and at
   room temperature

3 tablespoons cocoa powder

2 large eggs

³/₄oz dark chocolate

confectioners' sugar, for dusting

ice cream and raspberry coulis, to serve (optional)

Filling

1lb 2oz dark chocolate

³/₄ cup milk

1¹/₃ cups heavy cream

1 vanilla pod, split

3 eggs

Ganache

9oz dark chocolate

¹/₂ stick unsalted butter

1 cup heavy cream

1 tablespoon brandy

Nutritional value per serving:

Calories: 989

Fats: 70g

Carbohydrates: 82g

Salt: 0.31g

Sift the flour into a mixing bowl and add the sugar, butter, and cocoa. Blend together, add the eggs and mix to a firm paste. Chill for 1 hour, then shred the pastry into a flan pan evenly over the base and press down all over to form the base and sides of the tart shell. Finely shred over the dark chocolate and chill for about 20 minutes.

Preheat the oven to 350°F. Melt the chocolate gently in a bowl over a saucepan of simmering water. In a separate saucepan, bring the milk, cream, and split vanilla pod to a gentle simmer, then turn the heat to low. Crack the eggs into a large heatproof bowl and whisk lightly. Pull the milk and cream from heat. Continue to whisk the eggs while you pour in the milk and cream. Gently fold the melted chocolate into this mixture.

Remove the tart shell from the fridge, pour in the filling and place straight into the oven. After 5 minutes, turn the oven down to 300°F, cook for 10 minutes more, then turn the oven down to 230°F and cook for a further 20 minutes. Finally turn the oven off but leave the tart in there for about 25 minutes or so. Remove when cool.

Make the ganache: melt the chocolate in a bowl set over a saucepan of gently simmering water. Once it has melted, stir in the butter, remove from the heat and allow to cool for at least 20 minutes. Whip the heavy cream until just peaking and then mix in the brandy. Fold the cream gently into the cooled chocolate mixture, pour the mixture into a deep-sided baking pan about 8 x 16in and place in the fridge to set for about 20 minutes. Once the ganache has set, drag a dessertspoon along the top to form curls (one for each serving) and place on top of the tart. Dust with confectioners' sugar to serve.

ginger tiramisu

10 large eggs, separated

2¹/₂ cups superfine sugar

10 tablespoons boiling water

3 cups all-purpose flour

5 teaspoons baking powder

pinch of salt

2 tablespoons jasmine tea

1¹/₄ cups boiling water

1 tablespoon superfine sugar

¹/₂ cup ginger wine

1 tablespoon syrup from the crystallized ginger

finely shredded rind of 1 orange

2²/₃ cups mascarpone cheese

6 egg yolks

¹/₂ cup superfine sugar

4 tablespoons orange juice, strained

4 tablespoons ginger wine

3oz crystallized ginger, cut into small dice

6 egg whites

1¹/₄ cups heavy cream

Nutritional value per serving:

Calories: 965

Fats: 54g

Carbohydrates: 105g

Salt: 1.38g

Preheat the oven to 350°F. Oil and line two 11 x 14in Swiss roll pans with baking parchment. Whisk the egg yolks and sugar in a mixer until light and creamy. Add the boiling water slowly and continue to whisk for a further 5 minutes. In a bowl, whisk the egg whites until they form soft peaks. Sift together the flour, baking powder, and salt. With a metal spoon gently fold in the egg yolks then the egg whites, half at a time until well incorporated. Divide the mixture between the two tins. Cook for 20 minutes or until golden brown and springy to the touch. Remove from the oven and cool on a wire rack. When cool, cut the sponge in half lengthways, then cut 30 discs from it using a cutter slightly smaller than the glasses. The discs should be about ¹/₄in thick.

Infuse the jasmine tea in the boiling water for about 30 minutes. Add the sugar, ginger wine, ginger syrup, and orange rind.

Remove the mascarpone from the refrigerator ¹/₂ hour before you need to use it. Whisk the egg yolks in a mixer with 5 tablespoons of sugar, until light in colour and a thick consistency. Add the mascarpone, orange juice, ginger wine, and pieces of crystallized ginger. Whisk until creamy and smooth. Whisk the egg whites with the remaining sugar until they form stiff glossy peaks. Whip the double cream gently. Gently fold the egg whites, then the cream, into the mascarpone mixture. Mix in well.

Place 1 disc in the base of each mold, brush with soaking liquid then put 1 tablespoon mascarpone mixture on top of each. Repeat for all the sponge discs, finishing with the mascarpone mixture on top. Level off the tops with a palette knife. Cover and chill.

petit
fours

chocolate truffles

6oz best quality dark chocolate

2oz unsweetened chocolate

1 tablespoon Jamaica rum

³/₄ stick unsalted butter

2 tablespoons cream

3oz praline, finely crushed

melted chocolate and unsweetened cocoa
   powder for finishing

Melt the chocolate over a gentle heat to a thick cream with the rum. Draw aside, stir in the butter bit by bit, then add the cream and praline. Put small teaspoonfuls onto waxed paper. When set, have the melted chocolate ready. Put a little on the palms of the hands and lightly roll the truffles between them. Toss into a bowl of unsweetened cocoa powder. Brush off the surplus and put on racks to dry.

Nutritional value per serving:

Calories: 98

Fats: 7g

Carbohydrates: 7g

Salt: 0.05g

How to make chocolate truffles

stuffed dates

1 cup peeled pistachio nuts (reserve 1 nut for
each date)

1-2 tablespoons fragrant honey

1/2 cup ground almonds

25-30 fresh dates (approximately 3-4 per
person), stones removed

2 teaspoons orange blossom or rosewater

Place the pistachios and honey in a food processor and process at high speed until coarsely ground.

Transfer the content to a mixing bowl. Add the ground almonds and mix well. If the mixture is too loose add some more ground almonds.

Stuff a little of the mixture into each date, and decorate with a pistachio nut. Either arrange on individual serving plates on a pool of thick cream or serve in paper cases as petit fours.

Nutritional value per serving:

Calories: 83

Fats: 4g

Carbohydrates: 9g

Salt: 0.01g

halva

1¹/₂ cups superfine sugar

pinch of saffron strands

2 cinnamon sticks

1 teaspoon ground cardamom

1 cup olive oil

12oz semolina

6 tablespoons slivered almonds

¹/₂ cup honey

2 tablespoons whole blanched almonds

1 teaspoon ground cinnamon

Place the sugar and saffron in a pan with 2¹/₂ cups of water and bring slowly to a boil, stirring from time to time to dissolve the sugar. Add the cinnamon and cardamom, simmer for 5 minutes, then remove from the heat and leave to infuse.

Meanwhile, in a separate saucepan, heat the olive oil until quite hot, stir in the semolina, reduce the heat and simmer for 20 minutes, until lightly golden. Add the almonds and cook for 2 minutes. Strain in the saffron syrup and boil together for 5 minutes. Add the honey, remove from the heat and allow to cool slightly. Pour into an oiled and lined shallow pan, about 10 x 8in, smooth the top and set aside to cool. Cut into small squares, top each one with a blanched almond and dust with the ground cinnamon.

Nutritional value per serving:

Calories: 136

Fats: 7g

Carbohydrates: 19g

Salt: 0.01g

coconut custard

1 cup granulated sugar

1 cup thick coconut milk

1 teaspoon rose water

$^1/_2$ teaspoon salt

3 eggs, lightly beaten (use whites only, if you
 have some to use up)

Place the sugar and coconut milk in a large saucepan and heat gently, stirring until the sugar has dissolved. Stir in the rose water and salt. Add the beaten eggs (or egg whites) and fold in carefully.

Pour the resulting custard into a heatproof bowl or metal baking pan. Place in the top of a preheated steamer and cook for 30 minutes, or until set. Cut into small squares 1-1$^1/_2$in.

Nutritional value per serving:

Calories: 377

Fats: 14g

Carbohydrates: 61g

Salt: 0.94g

cherry tarts

Almond pastry

1$\frac{1}{2}$ cups all-purpose flour

$\frac{1}{2}$ cup ground almonds

1 tablespoon superfine sugar

$\frac{1}{2}$ teaspoon salt

1$\frac{1}{2}$ sticks butter

3 tablespoons cold water

1lb cherries, pitted (squeeze through the
   stalk end)

4-6 tablespoons superfine sugar (depending on
   the cherries' acidity)

juice of an orange and a lemon

1 teaspoon cornstarch mixed with a little water

2-3 tablespoons custard or sour cream

Nutritional value per serving:

Calories: 250

Fats: 22g

Carbohydrates: 35g

Salt: 0.56g

Toss the flour with the ground almonds, sugar and salt in a bowl. Cut the butter into the flour with a knife and then rub it in lightly with your fingertips until the mixture looks like fine breadcrumbs. Sprinkle in the water and press into a firm smooth ball of dough, still using your fingertips. Put the pastry aside to rest in a plastic bag in a cool place for 30 minutes to swell and gain elasticity.

Preheat the oven to 425°F.

Roll the pastry out with a floured rolling pin – use small light movements: the pastry is fragile. Use a wine glass or pastry cutter to cut rounds of the right size for your tartlet pans. Place the pastry rounds in the pans and prick the bases with a fork to prevent any bubbles forming. Bake for 15-20 minutes – the almond pastry will first whiten and then turn golden. Remove to a baking rack to crisp and cool.

Meanwhile, put the stoned cherries in a saucepan with the sugar and the juices diluted with their own volume of water. Bring to a boil, turn down the heat and simmer for 10-15 minutes, until the cherries are tender. Remove with a small strainer and reserve. Allow the syrup to cool a little, then stir in the cornstarch, reheat and bubble up for a moment to thicken.

Put a teaspoonful of the custard or cream into the base of each tartlet, arrange a few cherries on the top and finish with the thickened syrup.

guava cheese

2lb guavas

2 cups golden cane sugar

Rinse and roughly chop the guavas – skins, pips, and all – and put them in a roomy saucepan with enough water to cover. Bring to a boil and cook for 20 minutes, until the fruit is soft and mushy. Dump the contents of the pan in a clean cheesecloth and hang on a hook set over a bowl. Leave to drip overnight. Push the pulp through a strainer, discarding the skins and pips.

Put the strained pulp in a saucepan and beat in the sugar. Cook very, very gently for at least an hour until the pulp and sugar have formed a soft, dark, dryish mass, or spread on a baking sheet and leave in the lowest possible oven overnight. It'll set to a firm paste as it cools.

TIP

Wrap in paper and keep in a warm dry place – never in the fridge. Delicious with cheese.

Nutritional value per serving:

Calories: 20

Fats: 0g

Carbohydrates: 5g

Salt: 0g

MAKES 12

PREPARATION TIME: 10 MINUTES

COOKING TIME: 15 MINUTES

brandy snap baskets

1 stick butter

$^1/_2$ cup superfine sugar

4 tablespoons golden syrup

1 cup cake flour

juice of $^1/_2$ lemon

large pinch of ground ginger

clean small jars to use as molds

Preheat the oven to 350°F. Line a baking sheet with silicone paper. Gently melt the butter with the sugar and golden syrup in a pan, take off the heat and stir in the sifted flour, lemon juice, and ginger. Allow to cool. Drop generous tablespoonfuls of the mixture onto the sheet spaced well apart. They should spread into a 5-6in circle. Bake for 5-6 minutes or lacy and golden. Have the jars upturned ready to use as molds. Leave the brandy snap baskets to cool for a minute or so, then lift quickly off the tray with an egg slice. Shape over the upturned jars to form baskets. Cool on a wire rack. Do one sheet at a time or they will harden before you have time to shape them.

TIP

Fill with sliced bananas, butterscotch sauce, and caramel ice-cream, or with whipped cream and fresh fruit in season.

How to make brandy snaps

Roll the warm biscuits round the handle of a wooden spoon to make brandy snaps rather than baskets. Eat as they are or fill with whipped cream.

Nutritional value per serving:

Calories: 150

Fats: 8g

Carbohydrates: 21g

Salt: 0.21g

coffee kisses

3 cups all-purpose flour

1 stick clarified butter, softened (see TIP)

$^2/_3$ cup brown sugar

1 medium egg

2 tablespoons very strong black coffee

coffee beans to decorate

Sift the flour with a pinch of salt. Beat the butter and sugar until light and fluffy, then beat in the egg forked up with the coffee. Work in the flour to make a ball of soft dough – you may need a little more flour. Cover with plastic wrap and leave to rest in the fridge for an hour to firm up.

Heat the oven to 425°F. On a lightly floured board, roll out the dough. Cut out rounds and arrange on a buttered baking sheet, allowing plenty of space for them to spread. Dampen the coffee beans and pop one on each biscuit. Bake for 20-25 minutes until golden. Transfer to a baking rack while still soft and warm – they crisp as they cool.

TIP

Clarified butter, though not essential, gives a crisper result. To clarify butter, warm till it liquefies, then pour off the oil, leaving the milky residue behind.

Nutritional value per serving:

Calories: 121

Fats: 6g

Carbohydrates: 17g

Salt: 0.01g

brazil nut cookies

1 cup brazil nuts

1 cup all-purpose flour

1 heaped tablespoon cocoa powder

1/2 teaspoon baking powder

1/2 teaspoon salt

1 stick softened unsalted butter

1/2 cup brown sugar

1 egg, forked to blend

Reserve 18 of the best brazil nuts. Crush the rest to a coarse powder and toss with the flour sifted with the cocoa, baking powder, and salt.

Beat the butter with the sugar till light and pale. Beat in the egg, then the flour and nuts. The mixture should be soft enough to drop from the spoon, so you may need a little milk.

Preheat the oven to 375°F. Butter a baking sheet and sprinkle lightly with flour. Drop spoonfuls of the cookie mixture on the baking sheet. Using a damp finger, press one of the reserved whole brazil nuts into the middle of each cookie. Bake for 10-12 minutes. Allow to cool a little before transferring to a baking rack – they crisp as they cool.

TIP

The basic ingredients make the difference: choose a high-quality cocoa powder and crack the nuts yourself.

Nutritional value per serving:

Calories: 158

Fats: 11g

Carbohydrates: 13g

Salt: 0.24g

index

acknowledgments

The publishers would like to thank the following authors for permission to use the recipes reproduced on the pages indicated: **Darina Allen:** 26, 98, 102, 114, 118, 142, 144, 154, 166; **Hugo Arnold:** 22, 24, 80, 82, 146; **Ed Baines:** 30, 56, 86, 148; **Vatcharin Bhumichitr:** 60, 72, 160; **Maddalena Bonino:** 40, 58; **Conrad Gallagher:** 14, 32, 38, 70, 128, 130, 132, 140; **Paul Gayler:** 16, 20, 36, 52, 62, 64, 76, 88, 90, 94, 96, 100, 104, 106, 110, 112, 134, 136, 158; **Elisabeth Luard:** 18, 68, 116, 162, 164, 168, 170; **Alison Price:** 42, 50, 54, 124, 138, 150; **Oded Schwartz:** 74, 156; **Mandy Wagstaff:** 34, 44, 46, 48, 78, 108, 120, 122; **Sarah Woodward:** 28, 84.

The publishers would like to thank the following photographers for permission to use the images reproduced on the pages indicated: **Martin Brigdale:** 7, 9, 61, 73, 161; **Julie Dixon:** 75, 157; **Gus Filgate:** 15, 29, 31, 33, 39, 53, 57, 63, 65, 71, 85, 87, 89, 91, 107, 129, 131, 133, 141, 149; **Michelle Garrett:** 41, 59; **Georgia Glynn-Smith:** 1, 17, 21, 37, 66, 77, 95, 97, 101, 111, 113, 126, 135, 137, 152, 159; **Jeremy Hopley:** 43, 51, 55, 125, 139, 151; **Francine Lawrence:** 19, 69, 117, 163, 165, 169, 171; **Ray Main:** 2, 5, 12, 23, 25, 27, 81, 83, 84, 92, 99, 103, 115, 119, 143, 145, 147, 154, 155, 166; **Jean-Luc Scotto:** 70, 72, 74, 78, 82, 84, 86, 92, 96, 106; **Sara Taylor:** 35, 45, 47, 49, 79, 109, 121, 123